Peace and Blessings
with the Risen SON

William A. Booth

ISBN: 979-8-9891085-4-1 (Paperback Book)
       979-8-9891085-5-8 (eBook)

Cover Design & Published by Purposely Booked LLC. Printed in the U.S.A.

For information about the William Booth products and ministry, email us at debfbooth@gmail.com

The Dedication

I am dedicating this book to my family.
I married Deborah Booth, the love of my life, for thirty-
four years ago. Deborah has supported me in continuing
to look at the world differently in my writing. My
children, Kellie (Brentley) and William II (Lacey) have
been encouraging and supportive of my early morning
devotional development hours. They critique my writing,
challenging me to enhance my insight and writing style.
They always remind me that I have a church without
a building because you never know how many people
your encouraging words affect. Thanks for your loving
support.

William A. Booth

Acknowledgment

Dr. Cheryl Kirk-Duggan and Dr. James A. Holmes, two of my professors at Shaw University Divinity School, encouraged me to develop my writing style and to be creative. Since the initial devotional, I have written over 1600 devotionals and am still writing. Thanks for sharing your time and knowledge.

Introduction

Rise, shine, and give God the glory; see you at six. My
fellow soldiers would receive this message three times
a week in 2013. What started as an encouragement text
led me to write devotionals. The group (First Sergeant
Cliff Thompson (deceased), Master Sergeant Wanda
Lewis, Staff Sergeant Kendra Pickett, Staff Sergeant
Carnell Mickens, and civilian Marlon Wheeler asked
me to send them something daily. Since then, with the
strength of God, I have written many devotionals
that have blessed others. I decided it was time to
compile them and make them available to the world at
large. Now, I preach, teach, lead bible studies, facilitate
workshops, and write daily blogs. Thank you for joining
the community of believers ready to commit to the Lord
with an unrestricted YES! As you experience this daily
devotional, I pray your spiritual life is enhanced even
more. ***Peace and blessings.***

William A. Booth, MDiv

Purpose

People of any religion, race, gender, belief, political
ideology, or culture can read this devotional. This book
challenges an individuals spiritual relationship and
connection with their God. These writings are specifically
designed to help you achieve spiritual growth. While
reading them, I hope that you draw a connection and even
find that they speak to you directly.

How to Use this Devotional

Welcome to your 365-day journey of commitment to God!
This devotional is divided into four seasons with various
subtopics reflecting the different phases of life. Just as
life's seasons vary in length, you may spend more time in
some sections than others, and that's okay.

Read the daily devotional entry each day. Allow the
message to resonate with you. Stay flexible as you
move throughout the devotional. Embrace the process
and remain dedicated to your daily readings, trusting that
each entry is part of your journey with God. Expect to
be challenged and affirmed, allowing these moments to
foster growth and encouragement.

As you start this journey, remember that your
commitment will bring deep spiritual growth. Let this
devotional serve as a daily reminder that God is speaking
directly to you, guiding, and supporting you every step of
the way. Stay dedicated to your journey and have faith
that it will lead to meaningful change.
Peace and blessings.

A Fresh Commitment

Commitment is essential in anything you want to accomplish. As you engage in or move forward in changing your lifestyle, you must be dedicated to the challenges you may face. Trusting and obeying God will boost your ability to be steadfast and enhance your faith in God's unseen blessings. Commitment is not easy, but during this season, commit to trust, obey, and follow My instructions, teachings, and example. Your commitment and dedication to Me will change all facets of your life.

During this season, you will explore the following subtopics:

The Blessings of Commitment

Trusting and Obeying

Faith

The Blessings of Commitment

Day One

Sins of Omission and Commission

I hate any sin. You must investigate your life and work hard to avoid things that would create opportunities for sin to infiltrate. Let's explore two types of sin: sins of commission and omission. Sins of commission are sins you commit by doing something you shouldn't do. Some examples are all sexual sins: lying, manipulating, cursing, gossiping, slander, backbiting, theft, covetousness, murder, physical abuse, bullying, and mental abuse. Sins of omission" refers to the wrongs you commit by not doing something you should have done. This means it's not just your actions that can be sinful but also the things you fail to do. An omission is a sin that is easy to hide from others. Some examples are failing to pray regularly, failing to tithe, failing to help one another, failing to read and study the Bible, and failing to fellowship, etc. One thing is for sure: sin is sin, and I hate sin. Yes, you may fall short, but seek forgiveness quickly and renew or refresh your relationship with Me. Do not do the wrong you see others doing. Do what is right even when no one is looking. ***Peace and blessings.***

Day Two

Superstition And Black Magic!

I don't believe in superstition or want you to believe it. Superstition, black magic, or voodoo retain surprising power today because individuals believe in it. Some buildings do not have a floor labeled thirteenth. Most individuals will not walk under a ladder or cross a street if they see a black cat cross it. People will not split apart when walking around an object. Do you believe in "black magic," some magical spell? Are you one who requests a love spell to find love? How much did you spend to get it? Black magic and superstition go against everything I am about. Establish your belief in Me, Jesus, and the Holy Spirit; your world will be turned upside down with an enhanced relationship with Me. Blessings will fall from above. "But there was a certain man, called Simon, which before time in the same city used sorcery, and bewitched the people of Samaria, giving out that himself was some great one: "Acts 8:9 KJV) *Peace and blessings*.

Day Three

Make This A Great Day!

I am concerned about you and all you are trying to accomplish. Keep me informed, and I can help you through your day. Don't get frustrated if part of the process is delayed or goes wrong. Be fluid and accept changes so your day will continue to flow smoothly. Satan employs his angels and individuals to harass or spoil your day or activity. Stay prayed up. Continue to read and study the Bible for strength so you are not a soft target for Satan. If Satan attacks you, use scripture to defeat him and call on Me. I sent the Holy Spirit, your Comforter, to be with you all day. Listen to the Holy Spirit and enjoy a wonderful day. *Peace and blessings.*

Day Four

Your Sanctuary

A sanctuary is a place of refuge or safety. David was glad to enter the house of the Lord. During COVID-19, I know you are anxious and eager to return to your church. Since you have been out of the physical building, I see the true worship of Me in homes. Was the building a facade or a front where the outside world saw you go in and out? You did not worship while in the building and are not worshiping at home. Did you know I knew what you were doing? The physical church is not your Sanctuary. I AM. Did you forget that My Father built His church on me, Christ, and the gates of hell shall not prevail against me? I, Christ, am your sanctuary in your time of trouble. When you are in the storm, I am with you. I am your sanctuary when your money is low, especially when others choose not to deal with you. Call on me, and I will invite you in for shelter and protection. When you knock, I will open the door. Under my shelter, enjoy this incredible journey called life. I am protecting you. David said, "I was glad when they said unto me, let us go into the house of the LORD." Psalms 122:1 KJV)
Peace and blessings.

 Peace And Blessings : with the Risen *SON*

Day Five

Beatitudes

The Beatitudes are eight blessings I spoke on the mountain. Although spoken of years ago, they are valid today to bring hope to all you face. Individuals face many issues, and this passage of scripture in Matthew chapter 5: 3-11 (KJV) highlights an opportunity to bring hope and sunlight to dark situations. Blessed are the poor in spirit: for theirs is the kingdom of heaven. Blessed are they that mourn, for they shall be comforted. Blessed are those who hunger and thirst after righteousness: for they shall be filled. You can find comfort in these words. Just think how much comfort you have when you relate to me. I bring joy, happiness, peace, love, and more when you surrender your life and walk with me. I bring comfort to My true disciples. Try Me; you have tried multiple other things and are still in the same situation. I am waiting to hear from you so we can walk together. Remember, I will not leave or forsake you. ***Peace and blessings.***

Day Six

Where are you?

As you travel down this road called life, take a moment to think about where you are in Me. Now, I need you to evaluate where I am in you. I make Myself available to you so you can become engrossed in me. You find your attention drifting back and forth from earthly to heavenly, from sinfulness to holiness, this is a wake-up call. Stop straddling the fence and direct your focus, attention, and faith in Me, your Creator. As I have stated throughout my written word, "If you will be My people, I will be your God, and I will take care of you." I have not changed that thought or commitment to you. Where are you? Move closer to me so I may see and hear you. Talk with me, be My people, and make yourself known to Me so I can bless you. Move closer. ***Peace and blessings.***

Peace And Blessings : with the Risen *SON*

Day Seven

Ten percent!

When discussing tithing, most people want to know whether to give from the gross or the net. That is your decision, but which- ever way you do, be consistent. I only require ten percent. I can do more with ten percent than you can with your ninety. You are giving back to Me what is already Mine. In the Old Testa- ment, this offering went to the priest for them to live on since they could not farm or raise food for themselves. Today, your giving of ten percent is a test of your faith in, trust in, and love of Me. It goes to the church, but do not be overly concerned with how the money is used because "I will hold the pastor ac- countable" as I did the priest. When you give cheerfully, "The Lord is your Shepherd, and you will not have wants (needs)."

I will continue to open the windows of Heaven and pour you blessings in all areas of your life. "Bring ye all the tithes into the storehouse, that there may be meat in mine house, and prove me now herewith, saith the LORD of hosts, if I will not open you the windows of heaven, and pour you out a blessing, that there shall not be room enough to receive it." Malachi 3:10 *Peace and blessings.*

Peace And Blessings : with the Risen *SON*

Day Eight

Our Help

David looked unto the hills towards heaven, and his spiritual vision was elevated. He stated, "My help cometh from the Lord". Think about the type of strength that David must have had. Can you feel or see how he gained spiritual strength? It is hard to break a person whose spiritual strength drives them forward to a goal or to complete a task. I give my disciples that kind of strength. As disciples, know I am your aid, help, strength, power, driving force, and motivator that propels you forward despite your weaknesses. When you think you are weak, that is when you are strong because you are relying more heavily on me because you trust Me more. David certified Me God (as if I needed it) when he stated that I made the heavens and Earth. Special note: Yes, I made the heavens and the Earth. As disciples, you should know that your challenge today is trusting God. When you trust God, you are anchored. The more you believe in and trust God, the deeper your anchor digs, giving God's disciples spiritual stability. Wow, what a God we serve. Your help cometh from the Lord, which made heaven and Earth. Psalms 121:2 (KJV) *Peace and blessings.*

Peace And Blessings : with the Risen *SON*

Day Nine

Grace and Mercy

It is a beautiful moment when I extend grace and mercy, especially because it is unmerited. Unmerited means not deserved. My grace is unmerited favor, and it manifests itself through salvation. Grace is the manifested favor when I give you more than you deserve. Mercy is just the opposite. As I give you less when you actually deserve discipline. Your punishment could be death, but I gave you an illness instead. It's an extreme example of grace and mercy, but you get the point. When you ask for grace and mercy, you ask for "More and Less." Franklin D. Williams wrote the song. "Your Grace and mercy." "Your grace and mercy brought me through; I'm living this moment because of You. I want to thank You and praise You, too. Your grace and mercy brought me through." Grace and mercy are unmerited favors in distribution.

Allow My grace and mercy to save you from the punishment that is produced by sin. I have come to save you from the snare of the enemy. ***Peace and blessings.***

Day Ten

The Effect of a Ripple

Have you ever seen a ripple in a pond where someone dropped a rock? Life has a similar effect when you follow Me or continue as sinners. King David was on his rooftop when he saw Bathsheba, another man's wife, taking a bath. He desired her and sent for her. The two made love, and she conceived a son. God punished David with the death of that son. The ripple is the effect of David's sin and how it ripped his family apart. The ripple can extend for generations. There is a positive ripple of goodness when you follow My word. It does not mean bad things will not happen to good people. You must decide which ripple you want to produce. Review your journey and see the effect of your positive and negative ripples. Hindsight is twenty-twenty. What type of ripple will you create as you move forward in life? Remember, the choice is yours! ***Peace and blessings.***

Peace And Blessings : with the Risen *SON*

Day Eleven

Life is a Marathon

Have you ever run a marathon? My hat is off to anyone who tried or completed a marathon. Runners have shared that around the 19th or 20th mile, they feel like they have hit a wall or barrier. What a virtual obstacle to run into. Life is a race not for the swift Christian but for the one who can complete the entire race. Life is not a 10, 50, or 100-yard dash. It is a marathon, a long and enduring race for most. The wall can be a barrier, like family telling you to give up or Satan offering you a way out. Be sure you count the cost to finish the race and the price if you do not. Life is not a race for fast runners but for long-distance runners. Those who can overcome obstacles, barriers, family, friends, and Satan will be it for the long haul. I challenge you to make me proud of your endurance and watch how I reward your faithfulness. I believe in you! "And ye shall be hated of all men for my name's sake: but he that endureth to the end, the same shall be saved."Matthew 22:22 (KJV)
Peace and blessings.

Day Twelve

The Reward for Being Faithful

Job lost all he had and was left with his wife, his tent for shelter, and his life. Job maintained his faithfulness through all that he lost and the affliction to his body. He gained twice as many cattle and was blessed with money from friends. One of the messages from the life of Job is to trust and stay faithful to Me before the storm, during the storm, and after the storm has passed. It is during the storms of life that our faith sinks. It is easy to stay faithful during fair weather, but the storms test our faith and draw you nearer to Me (in most cases). If you can endure the storms of life, blessings come forth when the sun (SON) shines. Stay faithful to Me. I am a never-changing God before, during, and after your storm. ***Peace and blessings.***

Day Thirteen

When God Finds Favor

Haman devised a plan to kill all the Jews and to hang Mordecai, whom the King was going to honor for saving the King's life. Haman built a special gallows to hang Mordecai. Esther made the King aware of Haman's plan, and he hung Haman on the gallows he built for Mordecai. "The best-laid plans of mice and men will fail" when I intervene. As disciples of Mine, stay focused on your task, mission, and spiritual goal. Yes, there are (Haman's) individuals who want you to fail, but you are working under My plan and authority. I placed Esther in a position to intervene, and there are people or incidents in place to intervene for you. Trust Me and do what I have tasked you to do. If you do this, you will understand what it means to be in My favor. You will be blessed beyond measure. "And Esther said, the adversary and enemy is this wicked Haman. Then Haman was afraid before the king and the queen." Esther 7:6 *Peace and blessings.*

Peace And Blessings : with the Risen *SON*

Day Fourteen

Blessings Cannot Be Measured

The word measure determines a unit of measure, like a length, a width, a height, a weight, or a space of time. What method of measuring can we use to measure My blessings? There is no measurable tool or process to determine the length, width, height, weight, or time I used to bless you. What I do for My sheep is immeasurable beyond humanity's comprehension. My friend, I am "unfigure-outable." (Lol, new word) There's a song that says, "You can't beat God's giving." There is so much truth to this song. I don't know about you, but "BLESS ME, GOD, BLESS ME." I will not try to measure your blessing, but I will be ever more thankful and praise you for it. "Now to him who can do immeasurably more than all we ask or imagine, according to his power at work within us." Ephesians 3:20 (NIV) *Peace and blessings.*

Day Fifteen

Nehemiah's Prayer was Answered

Nehemiah prayed to Me for assistance in rebuilding the walls of Jerusalem, the great city. I showed Nehemiah's favor to King Artaxerxes, who gave Nehemiah letters for safe travel and reconstruction materials. As you read the book of Nehemiah, he faced challenges as other nations disagreed with the rebuilding of the wall. Nehemiah was My chosen person. He understood how to trust Me. He asked me for assistance getting this task completed. Regardless of the challenges before you, stay on task. The challenges are designed by Satan to discourage you or to slow you down. Do not give up; stay focused as Nehemiah did and take advantage of the challenges presented to you. "And I answered the King, "If it pleases the king and if your servant has found favor in his sight, let him send me to the city in Judah where my ancestors are buried so that I can rebuild it. "Nehemiah 2:5 (NIV) *Peace and blessings.*

Peace And Blessings : with the Risen *SON*

Day Sixteen

What If?

For what if some did not believe? Shall their unbelief make the faith of God without effect?" Since I am not a man but the creator of humanity, I do not get concerned about "What if." As humans, you want things to be perfect, to fall in place. God knows and understands what and who God created. I have allowed humanity to choose their direction, whether left, right, forward, or backward. Daily, you make a choice that may not be favorable to someone else. None of your choices changes My faithfulness to you. It would be great if you were as close to being faithful to Me as I am to you. Today's challenge is to stop the what-ifs and focus on a simple fact; "If God brought you to it, God would bring you through it." Paul tells the Romans that My faithfulness is not built or centered on the faithful or those who are unfaithful. Neither can anyone direct nor force Me to favor one or the other. Don't allow your unbelief or "what ifs" to hamper or control your faith in Me because I am not a man but man's creator. "What if some were unfaithful? Will their unfaithfulness nullify God's faithfulness? Romans 3:3 (NIV) *Peace and blessings*.

Peace And Blessings : with the Risen *SON*

Day Seventeen

Time Zones

When you do the research, there are more than twenty-four time zones worldwide. All time zones are not one hour apart; if so, we would have twenty-four time zones. There are locations whose time zone has a thirty or forty-five-minute offset. Ecclesiastes 3:1-8 reminds you that there is a time for everything, even in this world with more than twenty-four time zones. The reality is that I control time. Check this out! When I return, all time zones will see me simultaneously worldwide. Now, you understand the power I possess. And no one knows when I will return. Do not waste the space between one event and another (that is the definition of time). Prepare for my return by continuing to get closer to me daily by reading and studying your bible. No matter which time zone you are in or travel to, I am there because I will never leave my disciples. Remember, I love you all the time.
Peace and blessings.

Day Eighteen

My Father's Will!

These are the words I expressed to My Father. I was in agony on the cross, but I had to complete the task He gave me. I understood the assignment and refused to let Him down. I chose to say My will, but My Father's will. Yes, I made that choice even in a painful moment. As you deal with aches and pains from various ailments, illnesses, COVID-19, cancer, strokes, heart attacks, or diseases, consider it a blessing that you were selected so others can see the God in you. He will not put more on you than you can bear. You are going through your situation to be drawn closer to Him. Praise God in and through your pain. Squeeze My hand to relieve your pain because I have not forsaken you. "And he went a little further, and fell on his face, and prayed, saying, O my Father, if it be possible, let this cup pass from me: nevertheless not as I will, but as thou wilt." Matthew 26:39 (KJV) *Peace and blessings.*

Peace And Blessings : with the Risen *SON*

Day Nineteen

Committed!

Lord, You blessed me to exit one year and enter another.
I am starting the year committed to Your will and Your
way. Lead, guide me, order my steps every hour, and hold
my hand as we journey together. Redirect my sight and
control my thoughts as I continue my earthly journey.
Allow me to bless others with the knowledge and wisdom
you have given me. Allow the words of my mouth and
the meditations of my heart to be acceptable in Your
sight. Allow my words, actions, and deeds to balance
with Your commandments. Please help me to accomplish
the goals and plans You have for me. Lord, I know you
control everything; thanks for the protection, love, grace,
and mercy You give me daily. I do not take what You do
for granted because You don't have to do what You do
for me. Thanks for allowing me to be a recipient of Your
many blessings. With this commitment, I give myself to
You. Lord, may I walk with You from this day forward in
Jesus' name, Amen. ***Peace and Blessings.***

Day Twenty

Focus on Me

Pray this prayer with Me. Father I thank you for waking me up this morning. I thank you for placing the conviction in my heart to commit my ways and works unto You. I understand that if I do this then my thoughts will be established. (Prov. 16:3) So I understand that committment means I will give my all and focus on a thing. God I choose You. I choose to focus on You. Help me today as I navigate through situations and circumstances to not lean to my own understanding but to focus my eyes and heart on You. I choose You today, I choose Your will and Your way. I choose to focus and lean on You in all things. Even when things get tough, I will not allow anything to cause me to take my eyes off You. In Your Name I pray, Amen, ***Peace and blessings.***

Peace And Blessings : with the Risen *SON*

Day Twenty One

Immortality

Immortality is the ability to live forever or have eternal life. To be absent from the body is to be with Me. The natural body cannot survive in heaven. Even on Earth, the natural body has a living period. Then, it goes back to the dust. It will be a glorious day for this corruptible body to become an incorruptible body, and you are with Us in heaven. Special note to you: Run this race through the finish line, and do not assume you have won the race just because you are close to the finish line. Our desire is for you to spend your externality with Us in heaven. "So when this corruptible shall have put on incorruption, and this mortal shall have put on immortality, then shall be brought to pass the written saying, Death is swallowed up in victory." I Corinthians 15:54 (KJV)
Peace and blessings.

Day Twenty Two

Leave It and Follow Me

Do you realize how often you ask me questions, assuming the resolve will be easy? Then, you back away when the answer involves your participation because you anticipated minimal involvement. A wealthy gentleman had the same expectation, not knowing the magnitude of what he asked, and needed to prepare for Jesus's response. Can you or are you willing to sell all you have, give it to people experiencing poverty, and follow Me? The more things you have, the more things you cling to or that cling to you. Leave earthly possessions behind to enter heaven. You have the option to stay behind with your possessions. Your possessions cannot enter hell because even if buried with you, they remain on Earth. What I have for you in heaven is well worth giving up what you possess. Say goodbye to your worn-out possessions. "Jesus said unto him, If thou wilt be perfect, go and sell that thou hast, and give to the poor, and thou shalt have treasure in heaven: and come and follow me. "Matthew 19:21 (KJV) Read verses 16-23 to get the whole story. ***Peace and blessings.***

Peace And Blessings : with the Risen *SON*

Day Twenty Three

When to Call Me

Have you considered calling Me when the lightning flashes, the thunder roars, and the wind misbehaves? Have you considered searching for Me when the rain is pouring down and asking Me for directions? Call Me when you go through your midnight hours of grief, sorrow, and trouble. Call on Me when everyone else has turned their backs and love against you. Call Me when you have sleepless nights. Call Me when your money is short, and bills need to be paid. Call Me when death is knocking on your family's door. Call Me when your children do not respect you or when they are coming out of the closet. Call Me when your vehicle has left you stranded on the road. Have you ever tried calling on Me when there were no troubles or issues, and everything was calm and quiet? There is no specific time to call Me. Try calling Me at sunrise, noon, sunset, and even midnight. Call Me anytime, and I will be there. I am never late; I will always be there right on time!
Peace and blessings.

Day Twenty Four

Simon Says

I am sure you have heard of or played "Simon Says" when you were growing up. This game definitely develops your attention span. In this game, you can only do what Simon says; for instance, Simon says to turn left, and everyone should turn left. But when the leader says turn right, no one is supposed to move; the person who makes any movement is out. You really had to listen attentively! How good is your attention span? Simon says is a game, but you should use the same tools you learn in that game when I speak. The problem is that you hear what I say but need to believe it's sensible. Instead, you follow the advice of family, friends, and associates who suggest a different course of action. Just like in the game, you must move immediately when Simon speaks; that is how quickly you should move when I give you an instruction. You should know by now that I give guidance and instructions for your benefit, not your harm. Move quickly and follow My instructions. Replace Simon with Me, Jesus. ***Peace and blessings.***

Peace And Blessings : with the Risen *SON*

Day Twenty Five

Rooted And Grounded

Historically, the deeper the roots of a tree, the stronger the tree. I am using the verb meaning of root, which is to be established profoundly and firmly. Grounded means to be well-balanced and sensible. Trees can weather the storm when the wind and storms arrive because of their deep roots. Get rooted and grounded in Me before your faith gets tested. You will face many storms on your journey in life (problems with family and friends, at your job, at church, when traveling, and at home). Regardless of your location, the Holy Spirit assists you when challenges come. Stay rooted and grounded in Me no matter what your challenges are. I, your Shepherd, will ensure your safety and protection when you are rooted and grounded in Me. Read and study your Bible and watch how your life will change from the inside. "Let your roots grow into him and let your lives be built on him. Then your faith will grow strong in the truth you were taught and overflowing with thankfulness." Colossians 2:7 (NLT)
Peace and blessings.

Day Twenty Six

Following Instructions

It is incredible that when you instruct a child on things not to do, they seem to work hard to do what they are told not to do. Adam's instructions from Me were not to eat from the Tree of Knowledge of good and evil. Satan enticed Adam to go against My instructions. You must understand those instructions to follow them. What happens when you follow My instructions? Your journey becomes easier because you are doing what I instructed you to complete, and My blessings fall from above because what is for you is for you. Do not let others deter you or try to change the instructions to what they feel they should be. Repent and follow me. Obey My commandments. "But you must not eat from the tree of the knowledge of good and evil, for when you eat from it, you will certainly die. "Genesis 2:17 (NIV)
Peace and blessings.

Peace And Blessings : with the Risen *SON*

Day Twenty Seven

Common Denominator

Whatever happens in your life, you are the common theme or factor. You become the common denominator or interact with all facets of your life. Whether things in your life are good or bad, you are the center of all the action. What would happen if you allowed Me to become the common denominator, the center of your life? Would your life change? Yes, it would. Please allow Me to lead and guide you. What a significant change you would have in your life. When I come into your heart, you have a light that your soul sought, and now it's refreshed. When I come into your heart, you cease wandering and going astray from following your former sinful life and desires, and now your sins are washed away. With Me as your common denominator, beautiful changes will make your life worth living. Allow Me to be the center of your life.
Peace and blessings.

Day Twenty Eight

He Holds the Future

When you think about the future, you are thinking, wondering, or trying to figure out what will happen to you tomorrow. But when you exercise TRUST with Me, you do not worry about your future because you know I am your Shepherd. Real Christians live life in such a way that they can go with Me when I return to my church without a spot or wrinkle. Your love for Me should be so strong that you are killing your known sinful behaviors or habits daily so that you will be light enough to take flight with Me. Sin weighs you down mentally, physically, and spiritually. "Wherefore seeing we also are compassed about with so great a cloud of witnesses, let us lay aside every weight and the sin which doth so easily beset us, and let us run with patience the race set before us. "Hebrews 12:1 Trust and have faith in your Creator, who also holds your future. Your trust, faith, and praises drive Me to act on your behalf and allow you to be the recipient of My blessings. "Then you will delight in the LORD, and he will answer your prayers. Commit your future to the LORD! Trust in him, and he will act on your behalf." Psalms 37:4-5 (NET) *Peace and blessings*

Peace And Blessings : with the Risen *SON*

Day Twenty Nine

Life is a Journey

Your life is a journey on a road where you control your destination. Life has two-way traffic, with some individuals traveling in the right direction while others are purposely going the wrong way. The caveat to the right direction is that you're going in the direction of what you are looking for, even if others know it is not the correct spiritual direction. Your journey may have hills, valleys, rocky roads, uneven surfaces, and smooth roads. Although there may be challenges, fear not; Me, your Shepherd, will guide you through and to the right path; therefore, you will overcome your obstacles. You must make the best of your journey because you only get to travel once. Consider your journey a once-in-a-lifetime experience. My grace is with you while you're on this journey. "Consider it a great joy, my brothers, whenever you experience various trials, knowing that the testing of your faith produces endurance. But endurance must do its complete work so you may be mature and complete, lacking nothing. James 1:2-4 (NKJV)
Peace and blessings.

Peace And Blessings : with the Risen *SON*

Day Thirty

Benefits of Not Being Anxious

You have My peace beyond humankind's understanding when you are not anxious. I will guard your heart and mind, letting you understand that I am working on your behalf and love you. When you trust Me, you do what I tell you without doubting Me. Your words and actions do not betray your trust, faith, or belief in Me. Follow My instructions, trust Me, and walk with your Shepherd and provider. You can do all things through Me, who strengthens you. I will give you peace and provide for you. "And the peace of God that surpasses all understanding will guard your hearts and minds in Christ Jesus." Philippians 4:7 (ESV) *Peace and blessings.*

Day Thirty One

Woman, Thou Art Loose

"Woman thou art loose" are words made known to society by Bishop. T. D. Jakes, but Luke initiated this phrase. A woman with an infirmity of eighteen years was called by Me, who touched Me and said, "Woman thou art loose." Compassion is pity, sympathy, empathy, care, love, and more. I released her from her infirmity; how much more was she released from? When I free a person, they are free indeed. Why don't you let Me free you from infirmity, pain, heartache, situation, and much more? I am knocking at your door; open the door and let Me in and become free. "And when Jesus saw her, he called her to him, and said unto her, Woman, thou art loosed from thine infirmity. And he laid his hands on her: immediately she was made straight, and glorified God." Luke 13:12-13

Peace and blessings.

Day Thirty Two

When You Were a Sinner

What a powerful phrase! What an essential element of salvation is: The act that made forgiveness possible and made you "clean" in the eyes of Me, Jesus. Were you fully aware of the sins and stains you would inflict on yourself before you came to know Me as Savior? What is the effect of sin? Sin produces a ripple, affecting the lives around the sinner. I watched and shook my head since you did not take the way out that I gave you. You must allow the Holy Spirit to assist you with being saved from the habit and dominion of sin in your life. Take a piece of wood, drive nails into it, leave it for three days, and return. When you return, take a hammer, and remove the nails from the wood. When completed, you will see a perfect piece of wood, filled with holes, scared up, and no longer flawless. That is what sin does in and to your life. Serve Me. I died for Your salvation. ***Peace and blessings.***

Peace And Blessings : with the Risen *SON*

Day Thirty Three

Teach Me

Are you teachable like a child, or do you follow the proverb, "You can't teach an old dog new tricks?" For My Father to use you, you must be willing to open to new processes, procedures, and guidance from the Holy Spirit. In this scripture, David didn't ask for an easy path but a level or an even place of secure standing. When you trust and allow Me, I place your feet on solid ground to deter your slipping and falling. I can teach you to harness your words and attitude, change your personal view of things, and allow you to see through my lens. You must know, trust, and have faith in Me to follow Me. Once you begin following the Holy Spirit's guidance, your world changes from inside to outside. As this occurs, hold My hand, and walk beside me as I lead you through your journey with grace and mercy. "Teach me thy way, O LORD, and lead me in a plain path because of my enemies. Psalms 27:11 (KJV) *Peace and blessings.*

Day Thirty Four

The Roman Road

No one is righteous but Me. I died on the cross to give you salvation and a renewed relationship with My Father through Me. Accept Me as your savior and gain eternal life. These scriptures from Romans will guide you in leading someone to Me. Rom. 3:10, Rom. 3:23, Rom. 5:12, Rom. 6:23, Rom. 5:8, Roman. 10:9-10, " Rom. 10:13, Adam sinned while in the Garden of Eden, now everyone is a sinner. I sacrificed My life for your renewed, restored, and refreshed relationship with My Father. Share this message with others so they can have an opportunity for eternal life, evangelize, and lead someone to Me, Jesus. ***Peace and blessings.***

Day Thirty Five

An Extraordinary God

My Father is all-powerful and can do anything.
Extraordinary is something very unusual and remarkable.
Look at three scriptures of things My Father did above
your imagination and possible belief. 1) Time stood
still for one day (Joshua 10:13b, KJV: 2) He made the
water of the sea stop flowing for the Israelites to cross
(Exodus 14:21-22, KJV) 3) Birth of a child through a
virgin without human intervention (Matthew 1:18, NIV).
Wow, look at what My Father did, making the impossible
possible. Since My Father did all these things for his
people, what extraordinary things can He do for you?
Ask, and it shall be given to you; seek, and ye shall find;
knock, and it shall be opened unto you. Get to know Me,
accept Me as your Savior. ***Peace and blessings.***

Day Thirty Six

Don't Get It Twisted

Numbers 29:19 (NIV) says, "God is not human, that he should lie, not a human being, that he should change his mind. Does he speak and then not act? Does he promise and not fulfill?" I reveal myself to you daily, but you still do not know who I am. I am not a man, but I am the creator of man, and you continuously call Me the man upstairs. I do not lie, and I keep my promises. I created the universe, the galaxy, the moon, the stars, the sun, and all the planets. I carry you through your problems, sickness, financial situations, and much more, but you still do not know me. I told Moses to tell the Egyptians my name is "I Am." I Am all you need to survive this journey. You were created to worship and praise me of your own free will. How can you praise Me if you do not know Me? Do not get it twisted; I am God, not a man, not human, not the big guy on campus, or an imaginary figure. Although you cannot see me, I am real, all-powerful, all-present, and I process all knowledge. Get to know Me and disentangle your thoughts of who I AM. ***Peace and blessings.***

Peace And Blessings : with the Risen *SON*

Day Thirty Seven

Badge Of Honor

Acts 11:23c (NET) says, "Now it was in Antioch that the disciples were first called Christians." Before being called Christians, New believers were called "In the Way, Followers, Disciples, Brothers, Believers, Saints, Nazarenes, or Witnesses." Christianity was like saying Jesus-its" or "Jesus People. The title Christian was used to mock and harass you. Today, are you proud to be called a Christian? It should be an honor to have. Do you shrink away or conduct apologetics (defend the gospel of Me)? You should be proud to be one of my Followers, Disciples, Brothers, or Believers. Wear your title, Christian, like a badge of honor. You are the salt of the earth, seasoning the world with the good news. When you season the world, they become thirsty and will come to the well of living water. Hold your title of Christian like a light on a hill, leading individuals to Me by your life. Live for Me, and I will draw saved and unsaved individuals to me. *Peace and blessings.*

Day Thirty Eight

At The Name of Jesus

In the Old Testament, David recognizes the greatness of the name of the Lord. Oh Lord, how excellent is thy name? There is none like you on earth, in the earth, or above the earth. Excellent, meaning the best. NKJV) Philippians 2:9-11 "Therefore God also has highly exalted Him and given Him the name, which is above every name, that at the name of Jesus, every knee should bow, of those in heaven, and of those on earth, and of those under the earth, and that every tongue should confess that Jesus Christ is Lord, to the glory of God the Father." Not only is My name excellent, but mighty in that every knee shall bow, and every tongue confesses that I am Lord. Practice calling Me Lord now before you are forced. Praise Me, your savior, the name that makes Satan tremble, and Satan's angels find a hiding place. The name that brings healing, peace, restoration, comfort, and salvation. Get to know the excellent name and Me, the Son of God. ***Peace and blessings.***

Peace And Blessings : with the Risen *SON*

Day Thiry Nine

When the Roll is Called

"And I saw the dead, small and great, stand before God, and the books were opened: and another book was opened, which is the book of life: and the dead were judged out of those things which were written in the books, according to their works," Revelation 20:12 KJV.) When you stand before me, and I open the book of life, the things you have done will be exposed in the book. Your words, actions, deeds, and thoughts will be there. You have time now to change your lifestyle and enhance your opportunity to enter My kingdom. Accept me as your Lord and Savior so that the negative things will be seen but forgiven. Hold My hand now, and let's walk together for the rest of your life. This is also your opportunity to RSVP for your space in My Kingdom. Continue your preparation for My return. ***Peace and blessings.***

Peace And Blessings : with the Risen *SON*

Day Forty

Born Again

"Jesus answered, Verily, verily, I say unto thee, except a man be born of water and of the Spirit, he cannot enter into the kingdom of God," John 3:5 KJV Nicodemus came to me after dark, acknowledging that God must be with Me. I told him that he must be born again of water and spirit. This is a different birth compared to human birth. I made it plain that a man's first birth does not assure him of the kingdom; only being born again gives this assurance, a regeneration of sorts. You must make a metamorphosis, an inward change shown later in your outer behavior. Yes, I will do my work on you from the inside out. To belong to the heavenly kingdom, one must be born. Have you been born again? Accept Me as your Lord and Savior, and you have made the first step to enter my kingdom. ***Peace and blessings.***

Peace And Blessings : with the Risen *SON*

Day Forty One

Armor Up

"Put on the full armor of God, so that you can take your stand against the devil's schemes," Ephesians 6: 11 NIV. Do you have any idea what Satan has in store for you today? Of course, you do not, so you must armor up. On the battlefield, you must wear your armor! The enemy lurks behind hills, hides in the valley, and waits for you to come around the curve. He is looking for a weakness, a way in, and the moment you let your guard down, he comes ready to pounce on you and your purpose. Your armor has all the tools required to defeat your enemy. Remember, I am with you as well as the Holy Spirit. There are times you will fight the enemy, and there are times you will be told to stand still and let US (The Holy Spirit and I) fight for you. We have won the war; you are fighting mini battles as Satan is trying to bring others to the same destruction he will receive. Continue to wear your armor and fight your battles. ***Peace and blessings.***

Day Forty Two

I Dare You

"Taste and see that the LORD is good; blessed is the one who takes refuge in him," Psalms 34:8, NIV. When someone dares you, they are challenging you to perform an action to prove your courage. I dare you to open your Bible and learn of Me. I dare you to hold My hand and walk with Me. I dare you to call on Me before, during, and after your storm. I dare you to tell the world how I delivered you through cancer, COVID-19, your financial situation, and repairing your wrecked vehicle. I dare you to tell others of the healing you requested and received. I dare you to walk upright and blameless before your family, friends, colleagues, and peers. Yes, I dare you to tell your family, friends, colleagues, and peers that, unlike them, I love you unconditionally. I dare you to see for yourself the goodness of God. When you do not accept the dare from your friends, they call you chicken. When you do not accept a dare from Me, I call you foolish because you are walking away from the peace, blessings, grace, and mercy that only I can give you. I dare you to taste and see for yourself. ***Peace and blessings.***

Day Forty Three

Focus on Me

"For what shall it profit a man, if he shall gain the whole world, and lose his own soul?" Mark 8:38, KJV. Ten individuals on the internet are listed as the wealthiest people in the world. The first individual listed has more money than the combined gross domestic product of Myanmar, Laos, and Cambodia, which have around 76 million people between them. As you watch these individuals, they are miserable, chasing peace, happiness, a long life, and how to obtain more money. The love of money is the root of all evil. And again, I say unto you, it is easier for a camel to go through the eye of a needle than for a rich man to enter the kingdom of God. Do not let money or worldly things take your focus from Me, your Savior. Your mission is to praise Me and evangelize so others can find Me themselves. You are passing through this world to get to my kingdom. What you see as wealth and prosperity in this world is a mustard of what is in heaven. I look forward to showing you My kingdom.
Peace and blessings.

Day Forty Four

Perfection Through Christ

Matthew 16:18 (KJV) says, "And I say also unto thee, That thou art Peter, and upon this rock I will build my church; and the gates of hell shall not prevail against it." I called Peter the Rock. But Peter is not the rock that the church is built on. The church is built upon "The Son of the living God." Yes, I, Jesus, is the rock or foundation on which the church is built. I gave my life up and picked it up again on the third day, making salvation available to you. Peter's response was provided to him by the Holy Spirit. You are the Christ, the Son of the living God. Peter's and your mission are to seek the lost and present them an opportunity to accept Me as their Lord and Savior. The challenge is getting the unsaved to not focus on the physical church on earth. Once you become involved with it or touch it, anything you identify as perfect has lost its perfection. It is the same about an ideal church. It is through Me, Christ, that you can be perfected and make it to Heaven. So, do not hold others to your high standards. Your standards are not perfect.. Work to gain perfection through Me because I am the only standard you should strive to live up to. Work to become a member of God's perfect church. ***Peace and blessings.***

Peace And Blessings : with the Risen *SON*

Day Forty Five

Get Right with God

I will judge everyone by the authority given to Me by God the Father. Some do not believe in the resurrection of life or judgment, but God has forewarned you. Some individuals view society's judge and jury process as a joke, but I, Christ, is the jury and judge; My decision is final, and there is no appeal. Encourage others, but remind yourself to get right with God and do it today. Tomorrow is not promised because your tomorrow could be your today. I remember a song, "Get right with God, and do it now, get right with God, He will show you how. Right down at the cross, where He shed His blood, get right with God, get right, get right, get right." Enjoy your day in the Lord. "And he has given him authority to execute judgment because he is the Son of Man. Do not marvel at this, for an hour is coming when all in the tombs will hear his voice and come out, those who have done good to the resurrection of life, and those who have done evil to the resurrection of judgment." John 5:27-29 (ESV) *Peace and blessings.*

Day Forty Six

A Progressive Christian

Progressive is defined as happening or developing gradually or in stages, proceeding step by step. As Christians, we must take the proper steps or procedures to grow in the Lord. 2 Peter 3:18 "But grow in the grace and knowledge of our Lord and Savior Jesus Christ to Him be the glory, both now and to the day of eternity. Amen." To grow in Me, you have to read and study the Bible and spend quiet time with Me. Christians cannot remain stagnant or stationary in their spiritual thinking and actions. No, I do not change; you don't know everything about Me. You must read and study to learn of Me, which means you will grow in Christ. Don't become complacent by thinking you know enough about Me. Allow Me, through your studying, to remove the veil or your spiritual blindness so I can reveal more of Me to you daily. I reveal things to you according to your ability to understand. Expand your territory in various areas of your life, in your biblical studying, and watch your thought process change for the better. Progressive Christians look to improve or enhance their growth. As you get closer to Me, the greater your knowledge becomes.
Peace and blessings.

Peace And Blessings : with the Risen *SON*

Trusting and Obeying God

Day Forty Seven

Trust God

Trust in Me as an animal trusts its master. Trust is intricate, complicated, and complex as you deal with relationships regardless of physical or spiritual. Trust is giving or sharing with someone a sacred part of you. Trust is your firm belief in the reliability of someone or something. When you trust Me, Your Creator, you have placed your trust, confidence, and faith in your greatest available asset. Center yourself on Me in all things, watch everything fall in order, and enjoy your blessings. Be careful of what you share with friends. Not every person holds things in confidence as I do. Trust Me from whom all blessings flow. "It is better to trust in the Lord than to put confidence in man." Psalms 118:8 (KJV)
Peace and blessings.

Day Forty Eight

Be Not Dismayed

The world as we know it is full of events that can cause anxiety. Drive-by shootings are occurring day and night in any place. Individuals are shooting each other rather than talking it out and forgiving one another. Sickness and death are hitting all ages. But fear not or be displayed because I am still with you. I have things under control, as I did with Moses when he led my people out of Egypt. When you are at your weakest moments, I will strengthen you. Hold my hand as you journey through life, and I will comfort you. Hold my hand, and I will guide and give you peace that surpasses human understanding. Yes, being connected to me has benefits and blessings. Let's continue this journey together.: "Fear thou not; for I am with thee: be not dismayed; for I am thy God: I will strengthen thee; yea, I will help thee; yea, I will uphold thee with the right hand of my righteousness." Isaiah 41:10 (KJV) *Peace and blessings.*

Day Forty Nine

Can You Hear Me Now?

Hearing is an exceptional quality or tool given to humankind. It is used to listen to various sounds, whether by an instrument, machine, audio such as a radio, or the voice of a human. There may be many others, but you understand these essential items. Hearing something causes a reaction of determining what was heard or a gathering of understanding. When you hear spiritual instructions, you should be motivated to move swiftly and complete the task. What does it take for Me to get your attention? I speak softly but loud enough to awaken the dead if I desire. As a disciple, you must listen to My voice and move swiftly to complete your task. In times like these, I need My disciples to hear My voice and follow instructions. Can you hear Me now? If not, why not? He that hath an ear, let him hear what the spirit saith unto the churches. Revelations 2:7: "He that hath ears to hear, let him hear." Mat 11:15(KJV) *Peace and blessings.*

Day Fifty

Removing Barriers

A barrier is a wall, door, or anything that separates you from something. Some barriers are physical, while others are mental. The most challenging walls are mental. When dealing with people, we usually endure or are challenged by mental barriers. The individual places or establishes a mental barrier because of dislikes, hate, lack of respect, personal prejudices, etc. Barriers must be removed to gain the information, services, or, in this case, the healing required. Are you familiar with the healing of the ten lepers. They called on Me from a distance, requesting to be healed.

I said unto them, "Go, show yourselves unto the priest." And because of their obedience, they were healed. I was not close to the lepers but gave them a command and the ten lepers moved immediately. After seeing the priest, nine lepers went another way, and one returned to Me to give thanks. The story describes the man as a Samaritan, one who has differences with Jews. Even with his differences, he returned to the Jew and fell at his feet, praising him. I told the leper to "go thy way; thy faith has made thee whole." What barriers or walls do you need to remove? I tear them down daily for you. Trust Me and seek My assistance in removing walls or obstacles so that Satan does not bind you in hatred. I already paid the price for your precious freedom; enjoy it. Remember to return and praise Me. ***Peace and blessings.***

Peace And Blessings : with the Risen *SON*

Day Fifty One

What Would You Do?

In Daniel 3, King Nebuchadnezzar made an image of gold and demanded the nation and people to bow down and worship this idol when they heard the music play. Shadrach, Meshach, and Abednego refused to bow to an idol. They were thrown into a furnace that was seven times hotter than usual. When the servants checked, four men were in it instead of three. When the three men came out of the furnace, there was no evidence that they had been in a hot and smokey furnace!. The king worshipped their God. Today, many face issues of faith and what they believe. Do you have faith, trust, and belief that I will bring you through your trials? If not, read Hebrews 11 and consider all the situations I've delivered you through (sickness, court, family, jobs, church, and your issues). Thank you, Jesus. *Peace and blessings.*

Day Fifty Two

Following Instructions

Simon fished all night using his net and caught nothing. Jesus instructs Simon to launch into deep water and throw his net again. When you follow My instructions, you unlock an abundance of blessings. As I guide you today, listen, even if it does not make human sense. If you choose not to, you are limiting the successful life I desire for you all because you are unsuccessful in refusing to follow the instructions of your Shepherd. Goats disobey, sheep follow. God gave humankind free will to make decisions, but when God instructs, that is the decision for His sheep. Are you a sheep or a goat? "Now when he had left speaking, he said unto Simon, launch into the deep, and let down your nets for a draught. And Simon answering said unto him, Master, we have toiled all the night, and have taken nothing: nevertheless, at thy word, I will let down the net." Luke 5:4 (ESV)
Peace and blessings.

Day Fifty Three

Unbelief

The father comes to Jesus seeking help to have a demon cast out of his son. Jesus is troubled because His disciples couldn't do it. Jesus says, "All things are possible to him who believes." "Help my unbelief" is the father's answer. Unbelief is within each of us. You must recognize your weakness and ask Me for strength daily. Unbelief and a lack of faith go hand in hand. Disciples, walk with Me, talk with Me, listen to Me, and obey Me, and your unbelief will dissipate and be replaced by trust, faith, and a firmer assurance in the true and living God. I can turn your unbelief into a stronger faith in Me and enhance our spiritual abilities. "Jesus said unto him, If thou canst believe, all things are possible to him that believeth. And straightway the father of the child cried out, and said with tears, Lord, I believe; help thou mine unbelief." Mark 9:23-24 (KJV) *Peace and blessings.*

Day Fifty Four

Trust an Intricate Ingredient

Abram followed My instructions even when they went against his logical thinking. I instructed Abram to leave family and to go forward to a place I will show you. I did not give him the specific location but told him to go to a land I will show you. If I gave you those instructions, would you go forward or stay where you are? Your belief, trust, and faith in Me are tested as I challenge you to move out of your comfort zone to do more incredible things for Me and yourself. What is stopping you from following My special instructions? Trust is an intricate ingredient in your relationship with Me. I blessed Abram for his faithfulness, and you can be blessed also for trusting and enhancing your faith in Me. Trust and obey Me. "Now the LORD had said unto Abram, get thee out of thy country, and from thy kindred, and thy father's house, unto a land that I will shew thee:" Genesis 12:1 (KJV) *Peace and blessings.*

Peace And Blessings : with the Risen *SON*

Day Fifty Five

On a Mission From God

The Philistine Goliath challenged the Israelites to send one man to fight him. Only David accepted the challenge. Goliath's tools of war have killed men from various armies, while David's sling has rescued his flock from lions (no tigers) and bears. Goliath was a giant man standing around nine feet tall, while David was a young man under six feet. If you did not know the history, who would you support? A large army backed Goliath, while David was supported, covered, ordered, and under My authority. David is fighting a battle I presented and accepted it. I choose the battle; you fight and win because I have gone before you to prepare the way and the tools to defeat the enemy. If you trust and have faith in the unseen, move forward! Accept your God-given assignment and understand that you are on a mission from God. "David said to the Philistine, "You come against me with sword and spear and javelin, but I come against you in the name of the Lord Almighty, the God of the armies of Israel, whom you have defied." 1 Samuel 17:45 NIV) *Peace and blessings.*

Day Fifty Six

Jesus is Calling

Have you ever been awakened at night because you heard your name called and no one was there? Did you get up or pull the covers over your head in fear? Do not worry; you are not the first to have that happen to you.

I called Samuel late one night, and he answered, but he did not see anyone, so he returned to bed. The third time I called him, he replied, and we conversed. I call you at various times to get your attention. Sometimes, it is to warn you of an oncoming danger, and then I call you for a mission. Regardless of the call, answer, and let's enjoy our conversation. When you answer, be prepared for a mission. ***Peace and blessings.***

Peace And Blessings : with the Risen *SON*

Day Fifty Seven

Provision

The New International Bible explains the blessing God gave the Israelites while in the wilderness. Under normal conditions, clothes may have a five-year life cycle depending on the type of material. Fourteen thousand two hundred fifty days (counting leap year), I enabled My people to wear clothes and sandals that did not need replacing. Each day, I provided manna for food. Look at what I have provided for you. Can you see your blessings? Okay, do you have good health and a place to live: is your automobile in good condition? Are your children healthy and doing great? I continue to bless you even though you must buy clothes and food. Open your spiritual eyes and see the blessings you receive as you get under My care more. My message is, "If you will be my people, I will be your God, and I will take care of you." It's a simple message, but it's so true. Trust in My providential care and praise Me for the blessings you are receiving when under My care! Yet in My word, I said, "During the forty years that I led you through the wilderness, your clothes did not wear out, nor did the sandals on your feet." Deuteronomy 29:5 (NIV)
Peace and blessings.

Peace And Blessings : with the Risen *SON*

Day Fifty Eight

Rest

One of the most challenging tasks is to take a break
to rest. Rest is taking a break from all activities. You
schedule more daily activities than you can accomplish
and wonder why you are tired. Even on the day you
choose to worship Me, your mind is on the next event
instead of all your thoughts and energy being focused
on Me. Your thoughts are on eating, shopping, and other
events. Yes, I AM talking about you! Do you have time
for everything except praising your Savior on your day of
rest? I rested on the seventh day, why don't you? As you
rest, your mind, body, and soul will be refreshed when
you enter My rest. "For he has somewhere spoken of the
seventh day in this way: "And God rested on the seventh
day from all his works." Hebrews 4:4 (ESV)
Peace and blessings.

Peace And Blessings : with the Risen *SON*

Day Fifty Nine

Crazy Instructions

Why do you fret, get frustrated, or lose faith when things seem impossible? Do you remember the story of Joshua? He followed My instructions and crossed the Jordan River on dry land. Yes, Jordan, he crossed a body of water on DRY LAND. You should trust My instructions because I care for you so much that I prepare things for you before you arrive. Individuals may laugh like the Israelites who walked around the Jericho wall for seven days. On the seventh day, the wall fell. Continue to walk beside Us (Father, Me (Jesus), and the Holy Spirit) and enjoy the blessings We have prepared for your journey with Us as you walk into what We prepared for you. We do not need your help; everything is under Our control. Just hold Our hands, trust, and walk with Us.
Peace and blessings.

Day Sixty

I Am on the Way

In Mark 5:26 (NLT) 'But Jesus overheard them and said to Jairus, "Don't be afraid. Just have faith." Jesus was on the way to Jairus' house when a woman touched Jesus' garment and received healing from her issue of blood. A servant from Jairus' house arrived and told Jairus that he no longer needed to bother Me because his daughter had died. In this brief statement, I encouraged him to have faith. Faith is seeing the impossible, believing the impossible, and trusting Me with the impossible. Don't be afraid, words of comfort, words of encouragement, and words of possibility I will give you. His daughter was in a room when I arrived at Jairus' home. Everyone laughed at Me because he said she was asleep. I emptied the room except for her parents and a few disciples. I touched her hand and said, "Little girl, get up, and He said tell no one and feed her. Just have faith. It's a simple statement but a challenging task. Relax; you do not have control over anything but yourself. Believe, trust, and have faith in our Creator as you take one day at a time. Faith, believing in the unseen. ***Peace and blessings.***

Peace And Blessings : with the Risen *SON*

Day Sixty One

Trust in the Lord

"Trust in the LORD with all thine heart; and lean not unto thine own understanding. In all thy ways acknowledge him, and he shall direct thy paths," Proverbs 3:5-6 (KJV). As Christians and disciples, you are mandated to trust in Me. Yes, I ask you to trust in Me, whom you cannot see, and have FAITH that I will do what I promised. I do not lie. The challenge is not allowing society, humanity, or the world to dictate, control, and invade our spiritual connection. Your belief, trust, and faith should be deeply ingrained, fixed, or established in your heart. Isaiah 55:8 states, " My thoughts are nothing like your thoughts," says the LORD. "And my ways are far beyond anything you could imagine." God will direct our path when you acknowledge Me for who I am. He will lead us on the path to victory, which is to His kingdom. Because God has all knowledge, our trust and faith are imperative to activate His blessings and power. The world has less than a mustard seed of what God has in store for those who love, obey, and trust Him. *Peace and blessings.*

Day Sixty Two

Trust and Obey

"When we walk with the Lord in the light of his word, what a glory he sheds on our way! While you do his good will, he abides with you still and with all who will trust and obey. Trust and obey, for there's no other way to be happy in Jesus but to trust and obey." (John H. Sammis, author)

Trust is a firm belief in the reliability, truth, ability, or strength of someone or something. Obey is to comply with the command, direction, or request of you submitting to someone else's authority. The words to this hymn above are encouraging and a reminder that you must trust Me, your invisible and all-present God. No, you can't see Me, but if you have a relationship with Me, you can feel My presence. You must have faith in Me that you trust and believe in. I said blessed are those who believe and have never seen. Now faith is the substance of things hoped for, the evidence of things not seen. Yes, it is imperative that, as Christians, you trust and obey Me as the Holy Spirit continuously guides you. Enhance your trust and obedience. ***Peace and blessings.***

Peace And Blessings : with the Risen *SON*

Day Sixty Three

Your Exodus

Exodus is the departure of a lot of people. Exodus is also the second book of the Bible that tells the Israelites' journey from Egypt. How does this relate to you? Let's take a different approach. Your exodus is your departure from a sinful life to a life with Me as your Savior. Are you like the Israelites and lose faith when things are not in your favor while I am putting things in place for you? You ask Me for something, and My answer may be YES, NO, or NOT NOW. Can you handle my answer while I bring you out of something to something? When leaving a comfortable setting, situation, or relationship, you have the desire to look back at your former comfort zone because Satan reminds you of your past. Remember, what I have is always greater, better, and more challenging for your faith in Me. You have exited your former situation, location, relationship, and sinful self. Can you trust Me while you are in the wilderness on the way to the promised land? Trust and never doubt because I will bring you out. You have come this far by faith, confidence, and obedience. Continue to execute My plan for your salvation. ***Peace and blessings.***

Peace And Blessings : with the Risen *SON*

Day Sixty Four

Punished and Exonerated

Daniel 6:22 (KJV) says, "My God hath sent his angel, and hath shut the lions' mouths, that they have not hurt me: forasmuch as before him innocence was found in me; and also, before thee, O king, have I done no hurt." Daniel was appointed Chief President under King Darius because of his knowledge and wisdom. To Daniels's surprise, his appointment to this position came with a side of jealousy. Yes, some will be jealous of you because of the favor on your life. You may not understand it, but that is a blessing from Me. The other presidents and princes encouraged the King to sign a decree that no man could petition (pray to) their God or man for thirty days. However, it was Daniel's custom to pray three times a day and he was not about to stop. And because of his unwavering reverence for Me, Daniel was thrown into a den of lions. He still stood on his principles even at the expense of being cast into a situation that could end in his demise. The next day King Darius called for Daniel and was removed from the den, and his accusers and their family were thrown in. Whew! Daniel had faith and trusted Me for his protection. He was punished and exonerated. Don't you know that just as I protected Daniel, I will protect you? Do you trust Me no matter what? Trust and obey at all costs; I am worth it.

Peace and blessings.

Peace And Blessings : with the Risen *SON*

Day Sixty Five

Do You Trust Me?

Psalms 9:10 says, "And those who know your name put their trust in you, for you, O LORD, have not forsaken those who seek you." In the words of Psalms 9:10, "Those who know My name place their trust in Me, for I, the LORD, have never abandoned those who seek Me." David spoke of those who truly know Me, those who have a relationship with Me, and those who have been tested. They know Me because I was there to guide them through their trials. Trust, My child, is a complex and intentional part of your relationship with Me. Jeremiah proclaimed that blessings come to those who trust in the Lord. You trust in the solidity of a chair, the reliability of your automobile, and you trust that I will wake you up each day. Even though you cannot see Me, you place your trust in Me. Trust is not a vague concept or a mere possibility. It is a positive force, a tangible reality. It is a steadfast state of the soul and mind, a recognition of your own needs and of My ability to fulfill them. Do you trust Me, your Creator, the one who holds the keys to heaven and hell? Today I challenge you to lean into this trust, this firm belief in the promises I have made to you. I honor My word, and that you can count on.
Peace and blessings.

Peace And Blessings : with the Risen *SON*

Day Sixty Six

Trust In Me At All Times

Trust is like an icicle; once it melts, it is gone. But just like a liquid that melts away from the icicle if put in the right environment, it can be restored. I challenge you to be mindful of the state of your heart and mind today. Remember I will keep you in perfect peace as long as your mind is stayed on Me. It is all about your trust in Me. You have to choose to renew your mind daily so that your trust is not tainted by the businesses of the day. Trust in Me with all your heart, and do not lean on your own understanding. In all your ways, acknowledge Me, and I will make straight your paths. Trust is an intricate ingredient in your relationship with me. Take the time to be intentional with Me today. Increase your trust in me and watch it create a space for Me to show up like never before in your life. ***Peace and blessings.***

Peace And Blessings : with the Risen *SON*

Day Sixty Seven

Wait On the Lord

Psalms 27:14 "Wait on the LORD: be of good courage, and he shall strengthen thine heart: wait, I say, on the LORD." (KJV)

There are various definitions of wait. To stay where one is physically, mentally, or spiritually until a particular time or until something else happens. Waiting is challenging because each of you has an agenda or schedule. My schedule and timetable will not match yours. Get a grip on reality. I am in charge of putting things in place for you. Do not try to help Me because you will postpone things and get in the way. Learn to wait, be of good courage, and trust the process. Many of My promises bear an extended waiting date, but they are sure and infallible. Wait on Me through faith and prayer. If I promised it, you shall receive it. If you endure the waiting process, you will be blessed. ***Peace and blessings.***

Peace And Blessings : with the Risen *SON*

Day Sixty Eight

Disobedient Men

Deuteronomy 2:14 says, "Thirty-eight years slipped by from when we first left Kadesh-Barnea until we finally crossed the Zered Brook. By then, all the men who were once ready for battle had passed away in the wilderness, just as I, the LORD, had said would happen." I had sent scouts to survey the new land I had promised My people. Among the ten, two were brave, ready to step into this land flowing with milk and honey. However, the other eight managed to convince the people not to enter. These eight deposited fear into the hearts of the people. Their reluctance had consequences. I allowed all the men of fighting age to perish. Imagine forty or more men breathing their last breath each day during the forty years they have wandered in the wilderness. I have plans for each of you, My children. Your willingness to trust in Me will provide for you, guide you through life's storms and dangers, and bring you blessings you can't even begin to imagine. I promised your ancestors a land flowing with milk and honey, yet their descendants were hesitant, even distrustful, to step in. Yes, it's difficult to place trust and faith at the forefront of your life. But remember, history has shown us how I provide for My people.

Those who trust, have faith, and obey are blessed, while those who don't, well, they face the consequences. So, where do you stand, My child? Don't be like the men too fearful to enter the promised land. Walk with courage, believe with all your heart, trust in My promises, and have faith in what I have prepared for you. ***Peace and blessings.***

Peace And Blessings : with the Risen *SON*

Day Sixty Nine

A Prayer of Trust

Pray this prayer. God, I trust You. There are so many things that You have shown me about your trustworthiness. You have been consistent and accountable, and I come to You seeking peace. Teach me to trust You completely, leaning not on my understanding but on Your perfect wisdom. As I navigate life's uncertainties, help me remember that You are sovereign and work all things for good for those who love You.

Guide me in every decision, calm my fears, and deepen my reliance on You. You, God, are the perfect example of reliability, and I am honored that You care for me. Amen.
Peace and Blessings.

Faith

Day Seventy

Faith

I met a hemorrhaging woman who touched the hem of my garment for healing. It was a simple act of touching a garment, but power left My body to heal her. I asked the man at the pool of Bethesda if he wanted to be made whole. I told him to rise and walk. He picked up his bed and walked. Your faith in Me enhances your healing. I went to my hometown, but I could not heal them because they did not accept me as Jesus, the Son of God. They lacked faith in who I was. What about your faith? In times like these, you need faith in Me to be delivered from all sickness. You don't have to accept me as Jesus, your Savior and Healer. Continue in the condition you are comfortable in and enjoy your pain, suffering, and sinful condition. Extend your faith beyond your eyes and ears. All you need is a mustard seed of faith. It's not the quantity but the quality of your faith. It is up to you to extend your faith. "Faith is the substance of things hoped for but the evidence of things not seen." Mark 5:39-40 (NIV) ***Peace and blessings.***

Day Seventy One

Faith Pt 2

Faith is the size of a mustard seed. A mustard seed is about the size of the tip of a feather, if not smaller. When asked how much faith you have, it is a twofold question. Size can mean a number as well as the depth of your faith. It takes one mustard seed of faith (quantity) to move a mountain (quality). It's not the size of your faith but the degree or depth of your faith. When you tap into true faith, it can move a mountain, fix your problems, or heal your body. Do you have the faith to believe in the unseen? Faith is the substance of things hoped for and the evidence of things not seen.(Hebrews 11:1) Faith believes I will intervene to respond to your requests. Everyone who responded to having faith received their blessing. Do you have faith in the size of a mustard seed?
Peace and blessings.

 Peace And Blessings : with the Risen *SON*

Day Seventy Two

Where Is Your Faith?

There are times that I may ask the question before healing individuals: "Do you have faith?" Peter was asked the same question when he started to sink while walking on water with Me. Faith is one ingredient in your Christian walk that you need to expand on. I asked My disciples on the ship the same question: "Where is your faith?" Faith is seeing and believing in the unseen, but it is possible by and through Me because nothing is impossible for Me. You must first have faith in Me, whom you have not seen. My presence is felt physically, mentally, and emotionally. Faith is the ingredient that keeps Christians fastened to their spiritual belief. With that belief, I will return and give my children heavenly bliss. Continue to believe, trust, and have faith. May My grace be with you as you enhance and unleash your faith. "When I woke up, I rebuked the wind and said to the waves, "Silence! Be still!" Suddenly, the wind stopped, and there was a great calm. I asked My disciples, "Why are you afraid? Do you still have no faith?" Faith is the substance of things hoped for but the evidence of things not seen.
Mark 4:39- 40 (NIV) *Peace and blessings.*

Peace And Blessings : with the Risen *SON*

Day Seventy Three

Three Points Of Contact

When a person falls in a medical facility, the medical staff advises the patient to use three points of contact to get up. Three points of contact is a rule for entering and exiting a vehicle, working on a ladder, and climbing in and out of big trucks. Christians are imperfect and fall from grace, but to get up, you must use your three points of contact (Jesus, the Father, and the Holy Spirit). When you seek forgiveness, you must first ask, and then your relationship can be restored, and in turn, the Holy Spirit can be released to guide you. Most Christians are slow to get up for various reasons. It could be internal or external factors and even the opinions of others that cause you to hesitate to come to Me for forgiveness. Regardless of who knows, use your three points of contact, brush yourself off, and move on in life. If you see another fallen person, don't just watch them; help them up regardless of their spiritual status and learn from their fall so you don't make the same mistake. The faster you get up, the quicker your relationship is restored with Me. "Brothers and sisters, if someone is caught in a sin, you who live by the Spirit should restore that person gently. But watch yourselves, or you also may be tempted." Galatians 6:1 (NIV)
Peace and blessings.

Peace And Blessings : with the Risen *SON*

Day Seventy Four

Faith

Do you know how important faith is in your Christian journey? Faith is believing in the unseen, which also includes Me. You don't see me, but you experience and receive My protection daily. You should have faith in my ability to heal your body and infirmities, just as the blind man's faith influenced his healing. Where is your faith? Do you carry it in your wallet or purse, or maybe that is why you carry your Bible- to show your faith? Carry your faith in your heart, mind, and soul; make sure it is always with you. In times like these, you must not leave home without it. Let your actions, words, and deeds display your faith. When you have faith, you do not lean on your understanding. Now hold My hand and walk with Me. "Then he touched their eyes and said, "According to your faith, let it be done to you." Matthew 9:29 (NIV)
Peace and blessings.

Day Seventy Five

Blind Trust

So many individuals are suffering from various sicknesses. Blind Bartimaeus was healed because of his faith. Where is your faith? I forgot that "Pastor Pillow" has not heard you calling. Execute genuine faith and ask Me to heal you. Most of the healing by Me was made possible because of the person's faith. Faith is not allowing your belief system to be influenced by what you see. Faith can move a mountain! Pray for your healing (that's your petition), and trust Me. Praise Me for the healing (give thanks), and recognize God as the creator of all (that's worship). Your faith assists in the execution of your healing. Now, walk with Me. Faith, Trust, and Belief are partners that activate My hand on your behalf. "And Jesus answered and said unto him, What wilt thou that I should do unto thee? The blind man said, Lord, that I might receive my sight. And Jesus told him, go thy way; thy faith has made thee whole. And immediately he received his sight and followed Jesus in the way." Mark 10:51-52 *Peace and blessings.*

Day Seventy Six

According To Your Faith

Imagine having a condition from birth. It is one that you have had as long as you can remember, one that seems to be a part of your identity, and one that others even identify you as. It is a condition contrary to the plan and purpose I shared with you, but you are so used to having it that you are numb to its effects. You have had this condition so long that you do not realize all of the things you are missing out on because it has become your norm. That is what happened here with the Two blind men that Jesus healed. He had been healing people in the region of Capernaum. Two blind men followed Him and asked to be healed. You ask for healing, but healing is in conjunction with your faith. Conjunction brings two events together: the request for healing and the response needed to activate the request. The blind men had both components. Their healing was based on their faith. How much faith do you have in Me that enhances your worship and healing? These men chose to believe that I would do this for them. Their faith activated My hand! That is powerful. "When he had gone indoors, the blind men came to him, and he asked them, "Do you believe that I can do this?" "Yes, Lord," they replied. Then he touched their eyes and said, "According to your faith, let it be done to you." Matthew 9:28-29 (NIV) What would happen in your life today if you allowed your faith to connect with your belief?

Peace and blessings.

Peace And Blessings : with the Risen *SON*

Day Seventy Seven

Patiently Waiting

"The word patience in Hebrew is "qavah" which means "to wait for, to look for, to hope, or to expect." In Greek, it is often used as "hypomenō, " meaning "to remain, to abide, to preserve, endure, or to bear bravely and calmly." Patience is the state of forbearing or endurance under difficult circumstances (wikipedia.org/wiki/Patience). Patience is listed in the bible as long-suffering. If you do not have the patience to deal with individuals on this earth, you will not have the patience to deal with or wait on Me. Each has a different timetable. Some say, "That person got on my last nerve." Waiting on Me will get on your last nerve and then some. To have patience with Me requires faith in Me. I "am not a man" and will not lie. Patience, long-suffering, forbearance, and endurance are entangled in your faith. "Be still before the Lord and wait patiently for him; fret not yourself over the one who prospers in his way, over the man who carries out evil devices." Psalm 37:7(NIV) *Peace and blessings.*

Peace And Blessings : with the Risen *SON*

Day Seventy Eight

Let Your Faith Touch Me

Do you know how important faith is in your Christian journey? Do you treat it as something of value? Or as an accessory that can be disposed of. As believers, you are to carry your faith in your heart, mind, and soul; it must always be with you. When you have faith, you do not lean to your understanding. Now hold My hand and walk with Me. "Then he touched their eyes and said because you trust Me to lead and guide you into safe and purposeful places. Today, stretch your faith to believe that I can do above and beyond what you have hidden in your heart. Matthew 9:29 says it best "According to your faith, let it be done to you. (NIV) My friend, what will your faith produce today? *Peace and blessings.*

Day Seventy Nine

Let Faith Remove Doubt

"I won't believe it unless I see the nail wounds in his hands, put my fingers into them, and place my hand into the wound on his side." These are the words of Thomas, one of My disciples. Thomas was speaking what many others were thinking. They, like Thomas, needed to see for themselves to believe. What about you? Do you need to see to believe I rose? Do you need proof before you move in faith toward what I am instructing you to pursue? Some say seeing is believing, but faith believes without seeing. Do you see the electrical current that is producing power throughout your home? No, but the lights turn on each time you flick the switch. Do you see the force holding the sun and moon in the sky? No, but they both stay suspended in the sky. You have never seen me, my Father, or the Holy Spirit, but you can feel our presence. Replace your doubt with belief; have full faith in me; you will be blessed. Extend your faith and believe in the unseen. "Blessed are those who have not seen, and yet they believed. Extend your faith and believe in the unseen" John 20:29 (NIV). *Peace and blessings.*

Day Eighty

Do You Have Faith?

Having faith is a challenging virtue a Christian must display. Faith is a public display of your confidence and trust in Me. Unlike unbelievers, you can see and understand the importance of your spiritual connection to Me. Your faith may appear foolish to those who do not have the same core values as you, but you must not waver! Continue to position your heart and mind with your belief, trust, and faith in Me. "As a man thinketh in his heart so is he," Proverbs 23:7. Train your mind to choose to have faith in all situations, and displaying it will become second nature. It will not be easy to make this choice every day, but when you push through and show Me that your faith outweighs your feelings, I am confident you will trust in Me. *Peace and blessings.*

Day Eighty One

Weaker Believers

As you mature in your faith and grow in your knowledge
of Me, accept those Christians who are immature
spiritually. I give knowledge and understanding according
to a person's ability to absorb the information. Each
Christian's level of understanding is different. Some
Christians can only drink milk, others can eat meat, yet
mature Christians can eat meat and have dessert. Weaker
believers must read and study more and come out of their
comfort zone in their faith. Do not belittle, dismiss, or
disrespect a weaker believer. When you were like them,
stronger believers took you under their wing or as an
understudy to assist you in your spiritual growth. Now, it
is your opportunity to pay forward (instead of paying that
person back directly, you pass it on to another person).
Take a weaker believer under your wing and teach them if
they allow you. "Accept other believers who are weak in
faith, and don't argue with them about what they think is
right or wrong." Romans 14:2 (NIV)
Peace and blessings.

Day Eighty Two

When God Prepares a Way

Joshua 3:13, "As soon as the priests carrying the Ark of the LORD—the Lord of all the earth—step into the Jordan, its waters flowing downstream will be cut off and stand up in a heap." Why do you worry, grow impatient, or lose faith when things appear impossible? Joshua paid close attention to My words and crossed the Jordan River on dry ground. If you trust in My Father, follow His guidance, for He paves the way for you before you arrive. People may laugh at you, just like they did the Israelites who circled the walls of Jericho for seven days. However, on the seventh day, the walls crumbled. Continue to walk alongside Us—the Father, Me (Jesus), and the Holy Spirit—and relish the blessings We have arranged for your journey with Us. You'll find peace, blessings, grace, and mercy as you enter what We've prepared for you.
Peace and blessings.

Day Eighty Three

The Lord Will Make a Way

The hymn says, "Like a ship that's tossed and driven, battered by an angry sea. When life's storms are raging, their fury falls on me. I wonder what I have done to make this race so hard to run. Then I say to my soul, soul, take courage; The Lord will make a way somehow." Life is full of surprises. One day, all is well, and the next day, it seems like the sky fell in. Throughout this year, some of you have or will face real challenges. Because you are here, you survived. I know there was a time when you couldn't see the light of day because the load you carried was so heavy. Not only was the load heavy, but those all around you seemed to put their finger on it to make it feel heavier. It's frustrating to go through, and nobody appears to assist you. At least, that's the way it seems. Have you learned from last year's struggles that help was right before you?

Take My (Jesus) yoke upon you, and I will lighten your load as you learn, trust, and have faith in Me. I will make way for My people and never forsake you. Be encouraged. (Matthew 11:29-30) (KJV) *Peace and blessings.*

Peace And Blessings : with the Risen *SON*

Day Eighty Four

How Strong Is Your Faith?

As I journeyed towards Jerusalem, I met a man named Jairus, a synagogue leader. He approached Me and fell at My feet. He pleaded with me to come to his house because his twelve-year-old daughter was on her deathbed. In the midst of this, I felt something leave Me. I paused and asked, "Who touched Me?" Everyone denied it, and Peter pointed out, "Master, the people are crowding and pressing against You." I knew something was different. I felt power flow from Me. I insisted, "Someone touched Me." My disciples were confused because anyone could have brushed against me in such a crowd. Then, a woman stepped forward, trembling, and fell at My feet. "It was I," she confessed. She explained that the moment she touched Me, she was instantly healed. This woman had spent all she had in search of healing. Now, she had put her faith into action. Despite her ailment and the societal norms that barred her from crowds and worship places, she dared to believe. Hoping for just a touch of the hem of My garment, she found her healing the instant she reached out. I told her, "Your faith has healed you. Go in peace." How strong is your faith, My child? Like this unnamed woman, your healing and breakthrough hinge on your faith. It's not about the quantity of faith, like a handful of mustard seeds, but the quality of your faith. You believe and trust; now, let your faith grow. As your faith strengthens, draw closer to Me. *Peace and blessings.*

Peace And Blessings : with the Risen *SON*

Day Eighty Five

Faith as a Weapon

As a believer, you are armed with unique weapons that are more impactful than a knife and a gun. Your weapons are not carnal. They are sharper and more invasive than any military weaponry. You have intangible tools at your disposal that are effective and mighty, but you have to use them! Faith is a weapon that grows as you get to know Me even more. Your faith is developed as you encounter challenges and conqueror setbacks. James reminds you that it is the testing of your faith that produces endurance and trust Me, you will need that as you live this unpredictable life. I used scripture to defeat Satan, and you must do the same. Your ever-trusting, unbreakable faith gives you evidence of the invisible, spiritual world. Use your faith as a weapon and stay on the offense, attacking Satan before he attacks you. Use faith as your weapon and survive your daily battles with Satan.
Peace and blessings.

Peace And Blessings : with the Risen *SON*

Day Eighty Six

Trust

David knew this well when he said in Psalms 56:3 (NIV), "When I am afraid, I put my trust in you." Trust is a firm belief in the reliability, truth, ability, or strength of someone or something. It's an essential part of any relationship, a step beyond basic belief. Trust is that middle ground where you step into the unknown, totally depending on someone's reliability and integrity. It's the beginning of establishing your faith in the unseen. Do you believe I am a reliable God? Do you trust that I am acting in your favor? Do you believe I have already mapped out how you will grow and develop here on this Christian journey? Trust forms a bond in a relationship that takes it to another level. Trust Me as your Savior; your life will never be the same. Our relationship will grow rapidly and exponentially. You will walk with Me, talk with Me, and nothing or no one will come between us. It is time to expand your capacity trusting Me. ***Peace and blessings.***

Day Eighty Seven

Your Rock

Psalms 62:2 (KJV) says, "He only is my rock and my salvation; he is my defense; I shall not be greatly moved." David took a defensive stance, declaring Me as his defense, confident that he would not be shaken. Can you say that today? Where is your faith in Me as your defender, protector, or shield? You should be completely focused on Me for help, confident I will not disappoint you. You will face battles, and know that I am with you! You will face some battles, and when you go to raise your sword of the spirit, you will see that I have already won the war. You don't have to worry about sinking sand when you're attached to the Rock. Stand firm while holding My hand, and walk with Me.

Peace and blessings.

Peace And Blessings : with the Risen *SON*

Day Eighty Eight

Trust God

Psalms 118:8 (KJV) says, "It is better to trust in the Lord than to put confidence in man." This verse makes a powerful statement. Trust in Me, your Creator, as an animal trusts its master. Trust is intentional, complicated, and complex, whether in physical or spiritual relationships. Trust is sharing a sacred part of yourself with someone. It is your firm belief in the reliability of someone or something. When you trust Me, your Creator, you place your confidence, and faith in the greatest asset you have. Center yourself on Me in all things, and watch everything fall into order, and blessings unfold before you. Trust in Me, from whom all blessings flow. Peace, blessings, grace, and mercy. *Peace and blessings.*

Day Eighty Nine

Wait on the Lord

Psalms 27:14 (KJV) says, "Wait on the LORD: be of good courage, and he shall strengthen thine heart: wait, I say, on the LORD." Waiting has many definitions. To wait you must pause. This pause means staying where you are physically, mentally, or spiritually. To wait on the Me means tnot taking action until I release you. Waiting is challenging because you have your own agenda and schedule. But remember, My schedule and timetable will not match yours. Most of the time it is opposite of what you think. I am in charge and am putting things in place for you. Do not try to help Me because you will only postpone things and get in the way. Learn to wait, be of good courage, and trust the process. There are so many things that your season of waiting produces. Wait on Me through faith and prayer. If I promised it, you will receive it. If you endure the waiting process, you will be blessed. ***Peace and blessings.***

Peace And Blessings : with the Risen *SON*

Day Ninety

In Times Like These

John 14:1 (KJV) says, "Let not your heart be troubled: ye believe in God, believe also in me." You live in a time when the world seems upside down and crazy things are happening. As you listen to the reported events, the earth appears to be spiraling out of control. Let not your heart be troubled or in doubt; trust in Me, for I have control of everything. Hold to your faith in these troubled times. Some things occur to enhance your faith. Remember, you do not control anything but yourself, so ensure you do things that please Me. Believe, trust, and have faith in Me because I will not leave or forsake you. I will continue to be your Shepherd who protects, loves, and cares for you. Hold My hand, and let's walk together through these times. *Peace and blessings.*

Day Ninety One

Staying in Your Lane

New drivers often feel nervous and focus closely on staying in their lane. Staying in your lane is a concept that should be applied in more situations than just driving. Consider stepping out of your lane in everyday life. You're stepping out of your lane when you try to control a situation from the passenger seat or give advice without being asked. When you choose to do that, it can lead to clarity and understanding. 1 Corinthians 12:25 (KJV) says, "That there should be no schism in the body; but that the members should have the same care one for another." Confusion often arises when people don't stick to their roles, whether at work, home, or church. By staying in your lane, you help keep things clear and organized. When you petition Me and allow Me to lead and guide you, this will be less of an issue. Think about how staying in your lane can lead to less confusion and more peace. ***Peace and blessings.***

Peace And Blessings : with the Risen *SON*

Day Ninety Two

Use or Lose

Matthew 25:23 (KJV) "His lord said to him, 'Well done, good and faithful servant; you have been faithful over a few things, I will make you ruler over many things. Enter into the joy of your lord." The individual with the least was afraid of losing what was given to him; therefore, he hid it in the ground instead of investing it. I have given you gifts, talents, and abilities, but you are not using them. Step out of your comfort zone, step into faith, and use your gifts. If you do not use them, I will take your gifts, talents, and abilities and give them to someone who will use them. If you use them, you can gain additional gifts and talents. Your gifts will make room for you when you use them. Your work will display itself, and I will bless you. May the work you are doing speak for you. Ask the Holy Spirit to guide you in how to use your gifts, talents, and abilities. ***Peace and blessings.***

Day Ninety Three

Blind With Open Eyes

Helen Keller once pointed out a difference between having eyes and having eyes but not seeing. Let's think about this differently: sometimes, those who are blind can truly "see," while those with sight are often blind. This is especially true when it comes to spiritual matters. Blindness typically refers to the inability to see due to a disease, injury, or congenital condition. Spiritual blindness, however, is the inability to see Me and understand My teachings. In Exodus 32:25 (KJV), you see an example of this when "Moses saw that Aaron had let the people get completely out of control (naked), much to the amusement of their enemies." Here, being "naked" isn't about lacking clothes but about being exposed to their weaknesses and their enemies. In situations like this, someone physically blind may have better spiritual insight because they're not distracted by what they can physically see. Reflect on your spiritual sight: Can you see the hidden secrets, messages, and spiritual guidance I offer?

Reading the Bible is fundamental.
While you might not understand everything initially, you will have enlightening moments when you ask for My guidance. Try closing your eyes to listen to the noise around you; hear My voice. You might be amazed at what you have been taking for granted. With open eyes, be ready to receive the spiritual messages I send you. ***Peace and blessings.***

Peace And Blessings : with the Risen *SON*

Your Season is
Changing!

Embrace and Prepare for the Change

Posturing

This season focuses on the posture of your heart. Heart posture is everything! Are you taking a position of gratitude, praise, and joy because you live a surrendered life to Me? Holding My hand as you walk decreases the probability of Satan causing you to fall. As you walk with me, tell Me what's on your heart as we fellowship together. The more you talk to Me, the closer we become; in turn, others will see Me in you. Verbally express your appreciation or thankfulness and get your blessings.

During this season, you will explore the following subtopics:

A Postured Heart: Praise, Joy, and Celebration Living

A Surrendered Life

Gratitude: The Importance of Spoken Words

A Postured
Heart

Day Ninety Four

When Praises Go Up

I do not give you things just because you ask for them. There are many times you do not need what you ask Me for. As I sit high and look low, I can see down the road of your life and prepare the things you need before you arrive. All you have to do is stay on course and live a righteous life as best as possible. While on the course, Satan will try to turn you astray and offer opportunities to make you feel or think he has a better deal. Talk to and with Me as you encounter his challenges, and I will fight your battle and bring you through. Living on this Earth is a dress rehearsal preparing you to praise Me when you reach heaven. It is true when My Father hears your praises in heaven, and He sends blessings down. Regardless of what you are going through, praise Me from whom all blessings flow. Praise Him in the morning, noon, sunset, and your midnight hour. Your praise is a testament to my goodness. Don't you see that I am worthy? As you praise Me, watch all good things come into your life. ***Peace and blessings.***

Peace And Blessings : with the Risen *SON*

Day Ninety Five

Gratitude

Take a moment and think about the word gratitude. It is the state of being grateful or thankful. Gratitude is a thankful appreciation for what you receive, whether tangible (touchable) or intangible (untouchable). Some people are thankful for the slightest thing you do for them. They thank and praise you repeatedly. Then, some individuals only express their gratitude if they are entitled to the things done for them. Now that you see both ends of the spectrum, I want you to reflect on which end you are on when praising Me. Are you grateful, or do you think and believe I am supposed to do things for you regardless? ***Peace and blessings.***

Peace And Blessings : with the Risen *SON*

Day Ninety Six

Created to Praise

No matter how you feel, "Praise Me from whom all blessings flow. Praise Me, all creatures here below." Do you realize you were created to praise Me? Be grateful for your blessings even if you did not ask for them. Do not let the rocks praise Me just because you choose not to. Show gratitude in the morning, at noon, and the day's closing. Do not allow world events to control you when you praise me. When praises go up, blessings come down. Do not worry; non-praisers do not get hit by falling blessings. ***Peace and blessings.***

Day Ninety Seven

I Am Your Song

I am your song. I am the answer to the questions and problems you cannot solve. I am your strength when you are weak. I created a masterpiece. I am your keeper who abides with you daily. I am the comforter who comforts you when you have fears and doubts. I Am your protector from both earthly and spiritual enemies. I am bread and who feeds you physically and spiritually. I am your water, which allows you to drink from the fountain that never runs dry. I am your key, opening doors, humanity says you cannot enter. I am your guide who places your feet daily on solid ground. I am your deliverer who delivers you safely to travel to spread My gospel. Who am I to you, or do you know Me? To know Me, you can identify Me through your relationship with Me.
Peace and blessings.

Peace And Blessings : with the Risen *SON*

Day Ninety Eight

Be Still

One of the most challenging things is to wait on Me. You wait for Me while dealing with the death of a loved one, while waiting on healing and while waiting for directions, to name a few things. While waiting, you need to exalt Me, you know, to think or speak highly of Me while going through your situation. Being still means stopping things from ceasing for some time. Turn off the television, radio, cell phone, and social media to talk to Me. Listen to the birds, look at the squirrels running from tree to tree, and watch nature moving under the grace of My power. In these moments of quietness, you will find clarity and direction. You had to be still during your accident or sickness, listen to My remarkable voice, and grow closer to Me. As close as you thought you were to Me, you realized you were far from knowing Me during your stillness. There is so much you do not know about Me that I want to reveal to you in your quiet moments. Be still and know that I am God. Exalt Me more now than ever before and receive your blessings. "Be still and know that I am God" Psalms 46:10a (NLV).
Peace and blessings.

Peace And Blessings : with the Risen *SON*

Day Ninety Nine

Who Wants to Be a Millionaire?

Who Wants to be a Millionaire was a popular game show where participants answered questions to win money up to one million dollars. Individuals are playing the lottery to win millions of dollars. The lady with the issue of blood spent all she had to be healed. Finally, she tried Me. Walking down the street to Zacchaeus' house, a woman touched me, and I felt power leave me. I asked who touched me, and she came forward. She received her healing. Would you believe that you are a millionaire if you have your health? Those with money spend so much trying to get healthy or stay healthy. You may not have lots of money, but I have blessed you with excellent health as a sign of My protection, grace, and mercy. It may seem minor, but those with failing health would love to be in your place. Praise Me for your excellent health. Praise Me in the morning, at noon, and night. Praise Me from whom all blessings flow. "Heal me, O Lord, and I shall be healed; save me, and I shall be saved, for you are my praise." Jeremiah 17:14 (EVS) *Peace and blessings.*

Day One Hundred

Sovereignty Has Supreme Power or Authority.

I am the Almighty, omnipotent with all power. When you consider My power, do you not think I can handle your situation, no matter how small? As you become one of My disciples, My sheep, or take on the title of Christian, remember that I, your Shepherd, will guide you through your trials—be they sickness, pain, hurt, financial struggles, or any other tribulation. Walk with Me and experience the power and authority of My glory. Let the My word remind you that the God you serve is the G.O.A.T., the God of All Time. "Our God is in the heavens; he does all that he pleases." Walk with Me, trust in My eternal presence, and let Me steer your life towards My eternal truths. *Peace and blessings.*

Peace And Blessings : with the Risen *SON*

Day One Hundred and One

You Were Not There

"Jesus said to him, "Have you believed because you have seen me? Blessed are the people who have not seen and yet have believed." John 20:29 (NET) I showed Thomas the holes in my hands and side, inviting him to touch them for his belief. Thomas was not there when I first appeared to My disciples after I rose. You were not there to see Me turn water into wine, to see Me raise Lazarus from the dead, to see Me cure the man with the withered hand, or to see Me cure the ten men with leprosy. You were not present to see Me remove demons, to see Me beaten with a whip with cat tails attached, or to see Me nailed to the cross. I gave My life to redeem your lost soul. No, you couldn't be there, but do you believe, or are you like a doubting Thomas?

Blessed are individuals who were not present but believed. Do you believe, or do you have to see for yourself? Faith is believing without seeing. Where is your faith in My truth, dying and rising? I didn't make this up, but when I return, you will see for yourself. Until that time. *Peace and blessings.*

Peace And Blessings : with the Risen *SON*

Day
One Hundred and Two

A Resilient Christian

Resilience is the ability of people to cope with life's adversities, emerge stronger from these experiences, and withstand and adapt to hardships, including trauma. In short, one's ability to get up when beaten, stomped on, kicked, spit on, talked about, and walk through life's traumatizing situations. Yes, life presents you with natural challenges (death and sickness), artificial (broken relationships), or self-inflicted (not following directions). How do you endure these obstacles, problems, or situations?

In most cases, you need help greater than humanity. When Job faced these challenges, he praised Me despite the difficulty. Even though I allowed Satan to inflict this suffering upon Job, he did not curse Me, but he praised Me. Praise Me as you deal with impossible situations; I will bring you through. Why do you praise Me? You have no control over these events even when you know the outcome. You are now the recipient of my blessings because of your praise. Thanks for being resilient, one who got up when facing diversity.
Peace and blessings.

Peace And Blessings : with the Risen *SON*

Day One Hundred and Three

Are You Content?

Discontent is a lack of satisfaction with
one's possessions, status, or situation. Being content means
you're happy with your current state and don't need or want
anything more to maintain your happiness. What makes you
content, happy, satisfied, untroubled, thankful, and carefree?
Is it money, clothes, a new car, or the spouse of your dreams?
These earthly things will fade away or need to be replaced.
Paul states that he was content or untroubled regardless of
his circumstances. Why? Because he knew I was with him.
I am with you also. I will never leave or forsake you. When
you focus entirely on me, I can give you the peace, love, and
satisfaction you desire. I can provide you with contentment
beyond human understanding. When I am raised to life again,
you will know that I am in My Father, and you are in Me, and I
am in you. True happiness comes from within.

Allow Me to bring inner peace and contentment even in your
weakened state or in situations that will blow your mind. "For
Christ's sake, I am content with weaknesses, insults, hardships,
persecutions, and calamities. For when I am weak, then I am
strong." 2 Corinthians 12:10 (EVS) *Peace and blessings.*

Peace And Blessings : with the Risen *SON*

Day
One Hundred and Four

Seventh Word from The Cross

Today is Good Friday, my last day on this earth in the form of a man. My time on earth has come to its limit. Tired and weak, I am ready to complete my task. No one can take my life because I gave it up Myself. I am giving up my life and can pick it up again. I can't think of anyone better to give it to than My Father. I am doing something you cannot do, which is to give up your life and pick it up again. Accept me as your Lord and Savior when you have time. Time is of the essence; take advantage of it. I hope to see you soon. I must leave now. "Father, into thy hands I commend my spirit: and having said thus, I gave up the ghost" Luke 23:46 (KJV).
Peace and blessings.

Day
One Hundred and Five

Unchangeable Truths

Unchangeable truths are truths that do not change in time. These truths remain the same. Let's reflect on some of the things that are constants. I am the creator and controller of the universe. I do not change. I am the Son of God, the second person of the Trinity. I have all knowledge and power and am present everywhere. You are born, and you will die. These are unchangeable truths you will experience. You must keep these unchangeable truths at the forefront of your mind. I sent my son Jesus to become a sacrificial lamb for man's sins. Even if an individual does not believe this, it remains unchangeable. No other person could or can do what was done for humanity. Hebrews 13:9 says, "Jesus Christ is the same yesterday, today, and forever." ***Peace and blessings.***

Day One Hundred and Six

Worship

Worship is the feeling or expression of reverence and adoration for a deity (God). There is prayer (Lord save me; Lord helps me to pay my bills); there is praise (Lord thank you for saving me; thank you for helping me to get money to pay my bills); and there is worship (Lord thank you for being the only true and living God). Have you considered your style of worshiping Me? You were created to worship Me. Do you really worship Me or go through the motions? I do know the difference. Worship is something that captures my attention. What are you going to do differently today as you worship Me? Let your worship be unparalleled to others, be yourself, and be unique in your expression of worship. Praise and worship Me and watch the blessings flow.
Peace and blessings.

Day
One Hundred and Seven

A Healthy Heart

In the New Testament scriptures, the subject of circumcision continued to surface. Jews were physically circumcised, but the Gentiles were not. It is a Jewish custom that everyone is circumcised. They do not consider you a true Christian if you do not participate in that practice. However, I require that you - be circumcised through your heart. When you accept me as your Lord and Savior, you have chosen to allow me to cut sinful habits and ways out of your life. You have chosen to start living as a disciple.

Christian circumcision begins from the inside; it's a changing of the heart. Wow, changing your heart changes your ways, actions, and deeds. Making this essential inward change; sin will decrease, and watch your blessings flow. True circumcision is not merely obeying the letter of the law; instead, it is a change of heart produced by God's Spirit. And a person with a changed heart seeks praise from God, not from people. Romans 2:29 (NLT) *Peace and blessings.*

Peace And Blessings : with the Risen *SON*

Day One Hundred and Eight

Selah

'Selah' appears 71 times in Psalms and thrice in Habakkuk. It's found at the end of a verse and isn't meant to be read aloud. It's a cue to pause. For example, when you see a period at the end of a sentence, you don't say 'period'; you stop. Now that you have a better understanding of 'selah', why not take a moment to pause and spend time with Me? Find a tranquil spot, bring your coffee, sit down, and let's chat. Can you hear the birds singing, the rabbits rustling, or the squirrels scampering? Can you see Me at work in nature? Spending time with Me helps clear your mind of all its troubles. Remember how I would rise early while My disciples slept to spend time with My Father? This time with Me will rejuvenate and bless you as you unload your burdens and refresh your spirit with Me. So, smile, My child, because I love you. ***Peace and blessings.***

Peace And Blessings : with the Risen *SON*

Day One Hundred and Nine

Worthy is the Lamb

When John the Baptist was baptizing people, he saw Me, Jesus, approaching and declaring, "Behold, the Lamb of God." I was the sacrificial lamb sent from heaven to bear your sins and mend your relationship with the Father. I was the only sinless one worthy to be this sacrificial lamb. No human could have taken this role, for all had sinned. So, take a moment to thank Me. Thank Me for dying on the cross, for the price I paid. Thank Me for My love for you, for My nail-pierced hands. My death washed you clean, and now you can fully embrace forgiveness. "Worthy is the lamb seated on the throne." As John 1:29 (ESV) recounts, "The next day, he saw Jesus coming toward him and said, 'Behold, the Lamb of God, who takes away the sin of the world!'"
Peace and blessings.

Peace And Blessings : with the Risen *SON*

Day
One Hundred and Ten

Thank You, Lord

Pause momentarily and reflect on what I am accomplishing in your life. Remember, all power resides in my hands, voice, and thoughts. You reach out to Me, thanking Me for watching over you, even when you've made mistakes, which I call sins. You express gratitude for My help in picking you up and propelling you forward. You thank Me for healing your body when you're ill and for easing your aches and pains. You appreciate My unconditional love despite your shortcomings, a kind of love that humanity often struggles to offer. I ask you to reflect My love for others you interact with daily. Let them see Me in you. Your life has challenges but filled with peace and joy because you're walking with Me. May those you encounter be blessed through you.
Peace and blessings.

Day
One Hundred and Eleven

That Glorious Day

You have heard that I am returning for My church all your life. Every day, you see people going about their business and showing no concern for My return. That blessed and glorious day is closer than you would believe. I am just waiting for God the Father to tell Me to return to His church. I do not know the day, hour, or second I will return, but I will prepare. It will be a great day for some, so do not worry about what others are doing. You follow Me and my commandments. Stay focused on Me and not the things of this world. You cannot take the things of this world into my kingdom. All I need in my kingdom is your soul. So that you can get there, hold my hand, and walk beside me for the rest of your journey. "Looking for that blessed hope, and the glorious appearing of the great God and our Savior Jesus Christ." Titus 2:13 (KJV) *Peace and blessings.*

Peace And Blessings : with the Risen *SON*

Day One Hundred and Twelve

Praise the Lord

Praise is the expression of respect and gratitude as an act of worship: to express warm approval or admiration. As you journeyed through life, you faced many ups and downs, curves, valleys, roads with sinking sand, rocky roads, flooded roads, and uneven surfaces. Those roads represent various illnesses, deaths, job loss, family problems, drive-by shootings, dementia, and other problems in your life. Regardless of the road or obstacles, you overcame each challenging surface when you traveled with Me. Do not be like the nine lepers who did not return to say thank you. One out of ten recognized who blessed them. What about you? Have you taken the time to praise Me? Although I know the answer, this is an awakening question. Regardless of what you are going through, take time, praise me, and watch how you overcome your challenges. "Praise the LORD. Praise God in his sanctuary; praise him in his mighty heavens. Psalms 150:1 (NIV) *Peace and blessings.*

Peace And Blessings : with the Risen *SON*

Day
One Hundred and Thirteen

Mortal to Immortality

Every Christian should desire to meet Me in Heaven. The challenge lies in the understanding that you must pass from this life to reach there. Your current body is mortal, meaning it's subject to death. If it were to enter heaven as it is, it wouldn't survive; it couldn't meet the requirement of living forever. Only I can make that happen. 1 Corinthians 15:52 outlines how this transformation will occur. Can you see the depth of My love for you? I care for you so profoundly that I've planned precisely what you need to spend eternity with Me. To transition from mortal to immortal in the blink of an eye. As 1 Corinthians 15:52-53 (NIV) says, "It will happen in a moment, in the blink of an eye, when the last trumpet is blown. When the trumpet sounds, those who have died will be raised to live forever. And we who are living will also be transformed. For our dying bodies must be transformed into bodies that will never die; our mortal bodies must be transformed into immortal bodies."
Peace and blessings.

Peace And Blessings : with the Risen *SON*

Day
One Hundred and Fourteen

It is Praying Time

Repeat after Me. Most gracious and almighty God, hear the petition of your child. You present Me with new mercies, grace, and steadfast love daily. Forgive me for immorality and vices, which are rightly called sins. I live in a world where Satan always tempts me into sinful behavior. Put a hedge of protection around your child. Thanks for waking me up this morning in a warm home, putting food on my table, and for love in my heart. Have mercy on the names on the church's sick list and the names of the individuals that I think about. Bless the homeless people on the corner and living in tents. Forgive those pretending to be homeless. Each day, Lord, prepare me for that day and prepare that day for others. Hold our hands so we can walk with You and light our path so we do not stumble back into sinful conditions. Allow our lives to be sermons so others can see You living in us. Thanks for Your love, grace, mercy, protection, and the many blessings You give us. *Peace and blessings.*

Peace And Blessings : with the Risen *SON*

Day
One Hundred and Fifteen

My Prayer

Pray this prayer over your day. Our Father, which is in heaven, I need your assistance with the youth who have started school. Bless them as they adjust to a new school and new school year. Enlightening their minds will help them learn and develop as future adults. Protect them from gangs and anything that can harm or hurt them. As your disciple, I have faith in You, Lord, even if others do not exhibit trust and faith in You. It is the prayers of the saints that prevail much. This week, I am praying for others and placing myself on the back burner. Father. "Black lives do matter," as do all lives, and I ask for Your leadership in teaching, training, and guiding our youth to accept seasoned parents, disciples, and Christians' wisdom. I know nothing new under the sun exists, but they have not yet learned that. Thanks for protecting marriages and bringing peace to those relationships. If it is thy will, give healing to our sick and those in health care facilities, and have mercy to those who are in prison. Let this day be set to worship you in a mighty day of worship and fellowship. It is in Jesus' matchless name we pray, Amen. ***Peace and blessings.***

Peace And Blessings : with the Risen *SON*

Day
One Hundred and Sixteen

Rainbow In the Sky

Some days, you have quite a bit of rain. You must learn to enjoy the rain, especially since you have no control over the rain. However, you have control over how you respond to the rain that comes unexpectedly in your life. In Genesis, I became angry with man's sins and allowed it to rain for forty days and nights. Before the rain began, I instructed Noah to build an ark to house animals and his family. The rain covered the Earth so that nothing lived that was not in the ark. When the rain stopped and the water went down. Noah sent out a dove daily until the dove did not return because it found dry land. God made a covenant with Noah that the rainbow promises that He would never allow it to rain like that again. After a rain, you see a rainbow in the sky and are delighted to see its beauty. A sign of promise to Noah that also reminds humanity that I am faithful to My word. When you see the rainbow, know that it is a sign of commitment, that you can trust God for what he tells us, and that perpetual means as long as humanity exists. When we see the rainbow, the rain has stopped. *Peace and blessings.*

Peace And Blessings : with the Risen *SON*

Day
One Hundred and Seventeen

Prayer for Family and Friends

Pray this with me. Lord, I am thankful you woke me today to continue the journey. Lead and guide me as I walk in faith, trusting in You. Bless my family and friends. Thank You for watching over us, protecting us, and healing our bodies and minds. Thanks for our home, job, vehicles to travel in, but most importantly, Your Son Jesus, who sacrificed His life as a ransom for our sins. I worship You, God, because You are all-powerful, have all knowledge, and are all present. You are our creator, the author, and the finisher of my fate. Because I am connected to You, I know my fate is in the best hands. Protect those who are traveling from known and unknown dangers. Thanks in advance for hearing and accepting our prayer. In Jesus' name, Amen. ***Peace and blessings.***

Peace And Blessings : with the Risen *SON*

Day
One Hundred and Eighteen

A Prayer of Gratitude

Let's pray together. Lord, You continue to move in our lives in a mighty way. We recognize you as our creator, our God, and our savior. We know you are all powerful just by looking at the sky during the day or night. We know you have all the knowledge because there is no question we asked that you have not answered. We know that you cover all space because there is nowhere we can go that you are not present. We recognize and worship who you are and can sing "How Great Thou Art" with fervor or intensity and understood meaning. Continue to move in our hearts so we can become holy. Continue to open our intellect to understand your ways. Incorporate us more profoundly into your plan so we may continue serving and worshiping you. Today, Lord, our prayer is about you because we know you will care for our needs and protect us daily. Thanks for this conversation, and we are waiting to hear from you for additional guidance. In the matchless name of Jesus, Amen. ***Peace and blessings.***

Peace And Blessings : with the Risen *SON*

Day
One Hundred and Nineteen

Sweet Hour of Prayer

In seasons of distress and grief, my soul has often found relief and escaped the tempter's snare by Thy return, sweet hour of prayer! Meditate momentarily and enjoy the words to the song "Sweet Hour of Prayer." "Sweet hour of prayer! Sweet hour of prayer! That calls me from a world of care, bids me at my Father's throne, and makes all my wants and wishes known. It is in moments like these that allow God to bless you quietly. It is a time when you can steal away as Jesus did in the garden away from his disciples to spend personal time with God. Steal away from the hustle and fast-paced life presents us. Slow down and savor the moment to enjoy "blessed and holy quietness." Wow, now that was refreshing and relaxing.
Peace and blessings.

Peace And Blessings : with the Risen *SON*

Day
One Hundred and Twenty

TGIF

What is your breakdown of TGIF? In the social media world, this is "Twitter, Google, iPhone, and Facebook." We usually think of Thank goodness it's Friday or Thank God It's Friday, not bad. But Christians have other names that fit this acronym. Consider Today God Is First, or Thank God I'm Forgiven? Hopefully, you are optimistic and look at the positive acronyms. Acronyms are a part of our lives, and as you see, the same acronym changes within the different segments of our connectivity. But God does not change. God was the same yesterday; God is the same today and will be the same tomorrow. Acronyms change, people change, vehicles change, communities change, not God, who is faithful to us and never changes. Regardless of your acronym, thank God today and every day. ***Peace and blessings.***

Day
One Hundred and Twenty One

Invocation

An invocation is a prayer where you invite Me into the place where you conduct worship. It is not a prayer where you are praying for the sick and shut-in, the community's civic leaders, or the nation. You are inviting Me, but more importantly, asking if you may worship Me in this place because I am already present. Remember, I am everywhere already, and as you worship Me, you draw My presence. Have you conducted an invocation in your life, that is, invited Me in? Have you created space for Me? Although I am present around you, I must be invited in. Pray this prayer to invite me in, "Lord, I invite you into all facets of my life so that I can worship you everywhere I go because you are already present, waiting on my continuous worship." *Peace and blessings.*

Peace And Blessings : with the Risen *SON*

Day
One Hundred and Twenty Two

Midnight Praises

Pray this prayer over your day: In the quiet of this moment, I come before You, acknowledging that midnight is not just a time of day but often a symbol of our most challenging times. It is a time when the light of day seems hidden from us. I remember how Paul and Silas prayed and sang praises to You even in their darkest hour. Lord, help me handle my 'midnight' with the same faith and courage. Teach me to pause, reflect, and respond rather than react when faced with challenges. Inspire me to praise You, regardless of my situation. You had Paul and Silas' attention, Lord. Help me to give You mine. Remind me that praising You during my trials produces grace and mercy, just as it did for Paul and Silas. God, I praise You in all circumstances and open my heart to receive Your immeasurable blessings. As we recall the words of Acts 16:23-25 (KJV), "And when they had laid many stripes upon them, they cast them into prison, charging the jailor to keep them safely: Who, having received such a charge, thrust them into the inner prison and made their feet fast in the stocks. And Paul and Silas prayed and sang praises unto God at midnight: and the prisoners heard them." In Your holy name, I pray. Amen.

Peace and blessings.

Peace And Blessings : with the Risen *SON*

Day
One Hundred and Twenty Three

Spiritual Battle Prayer

Be offensive with your prayer today. Repeat this prayer after Me, Lord; I live in a world where individuals kill others for no reason. Their minds are programmed to kill if they think a person looked at them wrong or accidentally touched them. I now live in a self-centered world where Satan is exhibiting all his power to keep chaos, disorder, and confusion as a way of life. As a disciple, I know I am fighting a spiritual battle; therefore, I must stay tuned and focused on You, my Savior Jesus. Give me the physical and spiritual strength to sustain and keep me as I fight this battle. I know You have won the war against Satan. Please have mercy on my community, city, state, and nation as I continually engage in this spiritual war, a war unseen by the natural eye. Thank You for Your protection as I moved courageously to do Your will and win the battles You presented. Thank You for the many blessings You provide as I continue to love, trust, and display my faith in You. I thank You for being my Commander and God in this warfare. I will always honor and represent You in all facets of my life. In Your matchless Son's name, Amen.

Peace and blessings.

Peace And Blessings : with the Risen *SON*

Day One Hundred and Twenty Four

You Are Worth Saving

When you consider your former sinful life, you understand how my saving power pulled you out of rough places. You are so valuable to Me. You were worth sacrificing My life to save you. In this spiritual warfare, you are a precious commodity, valuable and desired by Satan, but more importantly, by Me, who offers you eternal life. If I thought you were worth saving, what does that tell you? I saved you from Satan, who has nothing to offer but death in a glorified package, a package made to look more than it is to persuade you into a sinful death. Accept what I have done for you and enjoy My grace, mercy, blessings, and unlimited love. Meditate on My love for you "because you were worth saving.
Peace and blessings.

Peace And Blessings : with the Risen *SON*

Day
One Hundred and Twenty Five

Advent

Advent is a period of spiritual preparation in which many Christians prepare themselves for the coming or birth of the Lord Jesus Christ. Celebrating Advent involves prayer, fasting, and repentance, followed by anticipation, hope, and joy. Many Christians celebrate Advent by thanking Me for My coming to Earth as a baby and for My presence among you today through the Holy Spirit and in preparation and anticipation of My final coming at the end of time. Advent begins on the fourth Sunday before Christmas Day, or the Sunday that falls closest to November 30, and lasts through Christmas Eve, or December 24. When Christmas Eve falls on a Sunday, it is the last or fourth Sunday of Advent. Prepare for the celebration and anticipation of My birth through prayer, fasting, and repentance, preparing for My glorious return. Allow the Holy Spirit to guide you through this preparation period and bring you into a more fantastic relationship with the Father, Son, and Holy Spirit.
Peace and blessings.

Peace And Blessings : with the Risen *SON*

Day
One Hundred and Twenty Six

I Dare You

When someone dares you, they challenge you to act as proof of your courage. I dare you to open your Bible and learn of Me. I dare you to hold My hand and walk with Me. I dare you to call on Me before, during, and after your storm. I dare you to tell the world how I delivered you through cancer, COVID-19, your financial situation, and repairing your wrecked vehicle. I dare you to say to others of the healing you requested and received. I dare you to walk upright and blameless before your family, friends, colleagues, and peers. Yes, I dare you to tell your family, friends, colleagues, and peers that, unlike them, I love you unconditionally. When you do not accept the dare from your friends, they call you chicken. When you do not accept a dare from Me, I call you foolish because you are walking away from the peace, blessings, grace, and mercy that only I can give you. I dare you to taste and see for yourself. "Taste and see that the LORD is good; blessed is the one who takes refuge in him." Psalms 34:8 (NIV) *Peace and blessings.*

Peace And Blessings : with the Risen *SON*

Day One Hundred and Twenty Seven

You Did It Again, Lord

Lord, you did it again. You called my name and allowed me to enjoy another day, and I thank you. Each day, You distribute grace and mercy to me. Another day to praise and worship You. Another day to tell the world of Your grace and mercy. Tell the world about Your healing power and the knowledge You shared with me. Another day to tell the world of Your presence and how I hold Your hand as I engage each day. Yes, I must tell the world of the joy and comfort You provide as I face the hills, valleys, curves, and unknowns that life presents. Lord, lift me when I am down, and You call me out when I am wrong. Like a "Father," You chastise me out of love, wanting me to do and be better. Thanks for being my Father, Savior, and Creator. No one can be or replace You as the only living God. Thank You, Lord, for allowing me to be a recipient of your love. ***Peace and blessings.***

Peace And Blessings : with the Risen *SON*

Day One Hundred and Twenty Eight

Removing Anxiety

Anxiety is Intense, excessive, and persistent worry and fear about everyday situations that are going to happen anyway. Anxiety in a man's heart weighs him down, but a good word makes him glad. In most situations, you worry about items, events, or situations you cannot control. There are at least three things in life you cannot control.
Time: You can't speed it up, slow it down, or stop it.
Weather: You can't make a sunny day, cause it to rain, make it snow all year, or enjoy the fall every day.
People: Stop playing games with people's minds as you try to control them; they will retaliate against you. Allow Me to give you another option to relieve your anxiety. Spend more time talking to me and watch your anxiety dissipate or fade away. When you walk and talk with Me, calmness will fill your spirit, and anxiety will disappear. Psalms 94:19 (NLT): "When doubts filled my mind, your comfort gave me renewed hope and cheer."
Peace and blessings.

Day
One Hundred and Twenty Nine

Prayer vs Praise

Prayer is spiritual communication between man and God, a two-way relationship in which man should talk to God and listen to Him. Prayer to God is like a child's conversation with his father. It is natural for a child to ask his father for what he needs. Prayer should be a daily process where one prays throughout the day. You talk to Me, telling Me of your needs, desires, and hopes. Praise is saying thank you. Someone opens a door for you, and you thank them in appreciation for their kind gesture. You ask me for a variety of things, and I respond, I answer, and you follow up with a thank you. Thank you, Lord, for healing my body, relieving the pain in my feet, and forgiving me of my many sins. Pray for your church; praise Me for your church. Pray for the sick in your church, neighborhood, and family, then praise Me for hearing and answering your prayer. Listen to Me as I respond to your request. Prayer is a two-way communication; you speak, and God listens; God speaks, and you listen. Read 2 Kings 20:1-11 to hear Hezekiah's request and God's response. ***Peace and blessings.***

Peace And Blessings : with the Risen *SON*

Day
One Hundred and Thirty

Praise God In Adversity

Psalms 35:19: "Many are the afflictions of the righteous: but the LORD delivereth him out of them all." (KJV)

Adversity is a state or instance of serious or continued difficulty or misfortune. In times like these, afflictions will invade your life in many ways. How do you handle challenges or adversity? Do you feel you are strong enough to manage it by yourself? When you go through by yourself, you feel like the world's weight is upon you. As disciples, as My children, allow Me to carry you through your challenges, problems, situations, or adversities. It does not matter if it is sickness, a financial problem, you need transportation, food on your table, or a place to worship. As long as you are one of My disciples, I will not leave or forsake you. Lean on and learn from Me. As our relationship grows, so will your blessings. Praise Me in your adversity, which helps you overlook your situations. Can you praise me when adversity attacks you? Come, sit down, pray, bow your heart, and watch your problems fade away as you continue walking with Me. *Peace and blessings.*

Peace And Blessings : with the Risen *SON*

Day
One Hundred and Thirty One

Worship as a Weapon

A weapon is a tool used for inflicting bodily harm and physical and spiritual damage that provides protection. Your battle is spiritual against Satan. You have a variety of tools to fight Satan, like prayer, bible reading, bible study, singing, Sunday school, and me (Jesus). Worship is showing reverence and adoration to God. Worship: Lord, you are the creator of heaven, earth, and humanity. You recognize God as having all power, knowledge, and presence. Satan was kicked out of heaven because he tried to take over. Satan and his angels fought against God and lost. Worship is a powerful weapon because you honor your creator, who fights your spiritual enemy. When at war, you must use every tool at your disposal. Using worship as a weapon changes your perspective, focus, and circumstances; it changes individuals around you and your enemy's position in your life. When you worship Me, you activate your greatest weapon, the Son of God. Nothing can go over, under, or around God's protection. Worship God, recognizing, honoring, and praising Him, and your world will change. ***Peace and blessings.***

Peace And Blessings : with the Risen *SON*

Day
One Hundred and Thirty Two

When The Storm Is Over

Mark 4:39 "Then He arose and rebuked the wind, and said to the sea, "Peace, be still!" And the wind ceased, and there was a great calm." Mark 4:39 (NKJV)

There was a great storm on the sea. My disciples woke me up, and I spoke to the wind and waves, which calmed the sea. Will you still know and talk to me when your storm is over? Do you seek and speak to me only when there are events in your life that you cannot handle? I created you and the storm to draw you closer to Me. September 11, 2001, was a national event that disturbed America. Millions of Americans called on Me for help. Now that America has recovered, the country that says "In God, we trust" no longer calls My name. They placed Me back into their "Matchbox" until another storm came. You can call on Me before, during, and after the storm because your matchbox cannot contain Me. Take my yoke upon you and learn from me, for I am gentle and humble, and you will find rest for your souls. For my yoke is easy, and my burden is light." I will not leave or forsake you before, during, or after the storm. ***Peace and blessings.***

Peace And Blessings : with the Risen *SON*

Day
One Hundred and Thirty Three

Beauty is Only Skin Deep

The Temptations sang a song titled "Beauty is only skin deep." Amazingly, the words in this song are very accurate. Your personality reveals what is in your heart. NIV) Matthew 15:19: "For out of the heart come evil thoughts—murder, adultery, sexual immorality, theft, false testimony, slander."

Beauty is only skin deep. Natural beauty comes from inside, from the heart. No matter how beautiful a woman is or no matter how handsome a man may be, if their heart is filled with sin, there is no beauty or handsomeness. The inner person defines one's beauty. The clothes, jewelry, shoes, makeup, perfume, or cologne are coverings for the outer person that can hide the heart until they speak. Allow Me to assist you in developing or redeveloping your heart. Listen to the Holy Spirit, who works to identify your shortcomings and faults, which are also called sins. Allow your inner beauty to outshine your outer beauty. Beauty is only skin deep, but natural beauty is displayed through words that protrude from your heart. Beauty is only skin deep. Hold my hand and learn of me as we develop real beauty that protrudes from your heart.
Peace and blessings.

Peace And Blessings : with the Risen *SON*

Living a Surrendered Life

Day
One Hundred and Thirty Four

Making a Change

Stepping into a new year is a blessing. Yet, nothing about your physical appearance has changed. True change, the kind that makes a difference, begins in the mind. It's an inward process. This internal shift must occur before any outward transformation can take place. Whether changing the colors inside your home, buying a new car, or altering a relationship, it all starts within the mind. Now that you're pondering this, what spiritual change or changes do you feel need My guidance? Let's begin with you finding a sacred space to spend time with Me. This sacred space is your sanctuary for reading, praying, meditating, and deepen your relationship with Me. The tranquility of the early mornings was always My preferred time for conversing with My Father. I would retreat to secluded places and pray. The disciples were asleep, the animals were silent, and the air was fresh. I will speak softly, but it might sound loud to you due to the quietness of the early morning. Empty yourself and draw closer to Me as we enjoy our sacred space and time together.
Peace and blessings.

Peace And Blessings : with the Risen *SON*

Day One Hundred and Thirty Five

A Virus Called Sin

Have you ever taken the time to think about what a virus truly is? Invisible and infectious viruses can only thrive inside living beings like us or other organisms. Now, think of the church as one of these living organisms. Just as a virus takes over a computer, spreading chaos throughout its system, sin can do the same within the church. And yes, it can begin with one unchecked person. I challenge you to use this as a reminder to fight off and defeat this virus called sin. Be sure not to become complacent. You are not immune to sin, but complacency will cause you to be vulnerable to its effects as you fight this virus called sin. Stay watchful because just as eager as I am to bless you, your enemy is looking to contaminate the plans and purpose I have laid out for you. ***Peace and blessings.***

Peace And Blessings : with the Risen *SON*

Day
One Hundred and Thirty Six

Asymptomatic

What does it mean to be asymptomatic? The definition of this word -is "presenting no symptoms of a disease." Yesterday, I talked about the virus of sin. Some people have masked their sin so well that they show no outward signs and walk around as if they are sinless. People may wear their masks and speak well, but they spread the virus of sin everywhere they go. Sin can be invisible or seen like a hurricane approaching. Asymptomatic people are dangerous everywhere they go. But I came to set you free. The choice is yours! Your mission is to repent, surrender, and walk with the Holy Spirit and me; we will guide you around the sins that can easily get you off track. As you walk with me, I will brighten your day and give you a fresh perspective on life. Asymptomatic Christians are dangerous to themselves and everyone they encounter. When you choose to follow me, it should be evident in your actions and how you show up in the world. Let the world know that God is real.
Peace and blessings.

Day
One Hundred and Thirty Seven

RSVP

How many times have you seen RSVP, that little request on invitations? Répondez s'il vous plaît, is a French phrase that means "Please respond." It's simple to tell your host, "Yes, I'll be there." Doing this helps ensure they have the right amount of food and sufficient chairs for everyone. Now imagine this: I, your Creator, have sent you an invitation, not just to any event, but to eternal life with Me. My RSVP? It's waiting for your response. Have you accepted Me, Jesus, as your Lord and Savior? Why wait? This isn't just about securing a seat; it's about where you'll spend eternity. Please respond to Me! RSVP to the most extraordinary invitation you'll ever receive. I think so much of you that I have chosen you the best seat in one of my best suites. I have prepared a place for you that I have set intentionally. And I am waiting for you to choose me, yes, for you to RSVP to me! Let Me write your name in the Lamb's Book of Life and prepare a place for you in My Father's house. ***Peace and blessings.***

Peace And Blessings : with the Risen *SON*

Day
One Hundred and Thirty Eight

Let Go and Let God

One of the most challenging things is relinquishing control of someone or something regardless of size. When you control something, you feel like you have power and are in charge. You tell individuals what to do who are dealing with a difficult situation. Now, someone is telling you your words, and you are challenged, giving every excuse possible to hold on to what you should let go. But when you give your cares and concerns to Me, you surrender your "power", anxieties, challenges, and utmost fear and worries. When you do this, I have your full attention and can move the mountains in your life.

Can you let go and let ME handle your affairs? Daniel, Joseph, Paul, and Peter did, and so can you. Trust is an essential factor in letting go. So, stop worrying; you cannot control most of the things you are worried about. Everything is under my control; therefore, let me handle your worries and care. Let go and let ME. "Give all your worries and cares to God, for he cares about you."1 Peter 5:7 *Peace and blessings.*

Peace And Blessings : with the Risen *SON*

Day
One Hundred and Thirty Nine

When Someone Does Not Change

Changing from bad to good is an option everyone has. It is an individual decision. People who desire to continue being sinful are given a reprobate mind, a mind where God rejects and curses their conscience (their moral sense of right and wrong). I allowed Lot and members of his family to escape Sodom and Gomorrah while the rest of the people with depraved minds were destroyed. Fire rained down from heaven to destroy both cities and their people because they would not change their conscience of sinful behavior. You may not be committing sexual sins, but sin is sin, and your behavior needs to change. I will work with you and guide you through transforming into a godly individual, but it is your choice. Give it some consideration.

"And even as they did not like to retain God in their knowledge. God gave them over to a reprobate mind to do those things that are not convenient;" Romans 1:28 (KJV) *Peace and blessings.*

Peace And Blessings : with the Risen *SON*

Day
One Hundred and Forty

To Abstain

Abstaining means restraining oneself from doing or enjoying something. In this case, it is the appearance of anything that is evil or, as Christians, anything that is against My will. A part of this process is to do nothing that will cause another person to sin. Abstain from the perception that what you do is evil even if you are not doing it. Some say a picture is worth a thousand words, but an image only sometimes displays what is true. Theologian Hiebert says, "The term form means 'that which is seen,' the external appearance. It points to the external form in which evil presents itself. I challenge you to shun evil in whatever form or appearance it may present itself." So, Christians must move from, run from, or turn from any known appearance of evil to avoid being trapped and to lead others from it. The Holy Spirit is a guide that will always steer you right. Allow Him to order your step, and you will do well. "Abstain from all appearance of evil." 1 Thessalonians 5:22 (KJV) *Peace and blessings.*

Peace And Blessings : with the Risen *SON*

Day
One Hundred and Forty One

Self Control

The Bible warns you that you will be slaves to what controls you if you do not have self-control. Whether it is food, lust, money, or words, you can be overwhelmed by the consequences of not having self-control. Remember, self-control is the foundation for living a righteous life that reflects Me, Jesus, and brings glory to God. You have the power to bring sin under control! Please do not allow it to control your words, actions, and deeds. Practice having self-control. It takes thirty days to develop a habit and seven days to break one. Work hard during the next thirty days to work on your self-control of one thing and add to it each thirty days. Having self-control is new for some of you. Call on the Holy Spirit and Me to assist you. Once we are yoked together, it will get easier. "Like a city whose walls are broken through is a person who lacks self-control."
Proverbs 25:28 (NIV)
Peace and blessings.

Peace And Blessings : with the Risen *SON*

Day
One Hundred and Forty Two

Removing Sinful Things

Do not take this literally. I am speaking about cutting off the things that cause you to sin. You can still sin with your left hand if you cut off your right hand. If your left eye is gouged out, your right eye can still sin – and if all such members are gone, you can still sin in your heart and mind. Bodily mutilation does not go far enough in controlling sin. You need to be transformed from the inside out. When you cut sin out of your life and work hard to remove it from your mind, you are worthy to enjoy a wonderful afterlife with me. Consider what will stop your entry into heaven and rid yourself of these problems. If you are not sure, consult the Holy Spirit for guidance. "So if your hand or foot causes you to sin, cut it off and throw it away. It's better to enter eternal life with only one hand or one foot than to be thrown into eternal fire with both of your hands and feet." Matthew 18:8 (NIV) *Peace and blessings.*

Peace And Blessings : with the Risen *SON*

Day
One Hundred and Forty Three

Find Your Sacred Space

Jesus' holy place or sacred space was the Mount of Olives—where he found quietness and could talk to His Father. Everyone needs sacred space to commune with Me. An undisturbed, quiet space, just you, nature, and Me. A screened porch, your empty mancave, your garden, and, for some, a bathroom are perfect places to meet Me. Have you found your sacred space? I get excited when you consistently prioritize My presence. If you have not already identified your sacred space, find it, and treat it as holy ground! I will always meet you there. ***Peace and blessings.***

Peace And Blessings : with the Risen *SON*

Day
One Hundred and Forty Four

Facing Adversity

Many individuals face adversity. Some call adversity "Bad Luck." During adversity, challenging situations, or events, friends may encourage you to go against your belief, just as Job's friends did. Satan's big lie is to tell you that no one else is suffering like you. Never think you are alone or the only one dealing with adversity. I have dealt with your adversity and many more. Call on me, and I will be with you through your challenges. Follow My instructions as we walk through them together, and your journey will become more manageable. You are not alone.

"Job faced multiple adversities and continued believing in, trusting, and having faith in God. (Job 1:13- 22).
Peace and blessings.

Peace And Blessings : with the Risen *SON*

Day
One Hundred and Forty Five

To Die Daily

We hear out with the old and in with the new as we enter a new year. Ironically, this is what I, Jesus say about accepting Me as your Lord and Savior. Kill your old sinful habits, bring forth the new you, and allow the Holy Spirit to provide you with positive habits. The Holy Spirit needs an empty and clean home to dwell in. Daily, it would help if you died by eliminating sinful habits that the Holy Spirit shows you. It does not matter how long you have been a Christian; daily dying is a necessary positive process. The more you empty your heart, mind, and soul of sins, the closer your relationship becomes. The closer you get to Me, the more intricate, complicated, and misunderstood things about Me become understandable. As you die daily to live forever, allow Me to continually clean your soul as you prepare to meet Me in the air.
Peace and blessings.

Peace And Blessings : with the Risen *SON*

Day
One Hundred and Forty Six

6th Word From the Cross

"It is finished." I said those words after drinking the wine vinegar. My journey on Earth is almost over. I had completed what my Father sent me to accomplish. As much as I wanted to give up, My love for you drove Me to hang on. Finishing a word that means completion; this task cannot be done again. My Father sent Me as a sacrificial lamb to die for humanity's sins. My father sent Me because I was sinless, and no human sacrifice could complete the reconciliation process. Man's relationship with My Father was broken, and now My sacrificial death will complete the mending process. But it's up to you to choose whether to accept My sacrifice. Many will reject it, and many will go to hell. Hell is real. Accept My sacrifice today because My Father will not do this again. We will meet again at the judgment, and hopefully, you will have made the right decision. "It is finished!" John 19:30 (KJV)
Peace and blessings.

Peace And Blessings : with the Risen *SON*

Day
One Hundred and Forty Seven

What Would You Invest in?

Do you remember the Bible story about the businessman searching for the most priceless gem in the world? At last, he located it and learned that it was for sale. But the price was outrageous! He would have to sell his home and business to buy that pearl and use every penny of his lifelong savings. The man's desire for that pearl was so deep and compelling that he did not argue about the cost. He only considered waiting once he could better afford the purchase. Nor did he attempt to bargain for a lower price. Immediately and eagerly, he hurried away, sold everything, and returned the money to buy the gem from the owners. The pearl represents eternal life, and those who desire it must be prepared to invest everything they have to obtain it. Eternal life is priceless but worth the earthly sacrifices to acquire it. Your prayers, bible reading, visitations, worship, bible study, choir rehearsals, prison visits, intercessory prayer, teaching, and preaching are not in vain. Peter said to Him, "Behold, we have left everything and followed You." Mark 10:28
Peace and blessings.

Peace And Blessings : with the Risen *SON*

Day
One Hundred and Forty Eight

Tomorrow, I will

James reminds you to be careful of what you say. You make plans as if you control today and tomorrow. You will do this or that; tomorrow, you will go to Jamaica. You live in a world where "Me, Myself, and I" is the center of everything. Most individuals take for granted that tomorrow will come. Some believe that they will live a long life. Some take their daily existence as if it is supposed to be. Do you make plans as if tomorrow will come? James tells us to say "if it is the Lord's will" because God controls everything. The rich man said, "This is what I'll do. I will tear down my barns, build bigger ones, and store my surplus grain there." But His soul was called that night. The lesson: You should live each day for God as if it's your last because you never know when My Father will call you home. Do not take your existence and time for granted. "Instead, you should say, "If the Lord wills, we will live and do this or that." James 4:15 (HCSB) *Peace and blessings.*

Day
One Hundred and Forty Nine

Which Road Are You On?

When moving from point A to B, you usually take well-worn routes. Have you ever considered taking a less-used route? The road, journey, or life you live to get to heaven is a less preferred route for Christians. Most tourists travel the route where friends, colleagues, and family members travel, and it is the desired road. But when you take the less utilized road, there are persecution, accusations, and insensitive and unforgiving individuals on this road. Yet it would be best if you held your peace. Do not be afraid to take the road less traveled. The other road has all the pleasures life on earth has to offer. But the less utilized road has life after death with an out-of- the-world experience called eternal life. I look forward to seeing you on the road less traveled.

"Enter through the narrow gate. For wide is the gate, broad is the road that leads to destruction, and many enter through it. But small is the gate and narrow the road that leads to life, and only a few find it." Matthew 7:13-14 (NIV)
Peace and blessings.

Peace And Blessings : with the Risen *SON*

Day
One Hundred and Fifty

What would you do?

Do you recall the bracelet sold years ago to encourage you to make good choices? Yes, that WWJD bracelet got many people out of sticky situations. As you read your Bible, you see the things I did, but more importantly, did you notice the results? People were healed, some surrendered their souls, and some received their requested blessings. But did you notice the opposition I faced? Have you counted the cost of doing things the way I did them? Are you willing to be ostracized by religious and political leaders? Paying for what the Holy Spirit directs you is a cost. If you want to be one of my disciples, there is a cost to pay. It would be best to count the cost before committing to things. This will help you only to do things you value or are willing to suffer for. These are things you are willing to pay the cost for. Therefore, please consider the cost before crossing the line. Once you cross over, the spiritual war is on. Are you ready to cross over into the life I predestined for you? *Peace and blessings.*

Day
One Hundred and Fifty One

Don't Sell Yourself Short

Many individuals sold their souls to Satan so they could enjoy the pleasures of this world. Their love for money is their driving force. When you look around, people have beautiful homes and luxury cars and do not lack anything; please don't be fooled into thinking it is easy. Never desire to have what another person has or be like them. You would be setting yourself up to be a target for Satan to bargain for your soul. He will offer you anything you want to get your soul to perish with him in hell when I return. I will return for my disciples, my Christians who sacrificed so much to go to my home called heaven. There is so much more in heaven for you than those who die and go to hell. Revelation 21-22 gives a snapshot of what's in heaven. Read both chapters to see why you may suffer on earth to have the beautiful things and pleasures of heaven. Live a righteous life and work to enter my kingdom. Looking forward to seeing you. *Peace and blessings.*

Peace And Blessings : with the Risen *SON*

Day
One Hundred and Fifty Two

Knock, Knock

I am talking to you, the owner of the door without knobs, so you control who enters. The door is the gateway to your heart. I stand and knock on a door I can easily open, but you must permit Me to enter your heart, mind, and soul. " You must open the door for Me to gain entry. If you don't let Me in, you lose so much that I have to offer you. But, if you open the door and give Me access to your heart, I will come into you and fellowship with you, and you with me. Wow, what a wonderful time of fellowship We would have. Knock, knock.

"Behold, I stand at the door, and knock: if any man hears my voice, and open the door, I will come into him, "Revelation 3:20 (KJV).
Peace and blessings.

Peace And Blessings : with the Risen *SON*

Day
One Hundred and Fifty Three

Dealing with a Beggar

Beggars are not new; other scriptures speak of beggars in various locations throughout the Bible. Peter and John encountered a beggar at the temple gate. When I discovered this beggar named Bartimaeus, I asked, "What do you want me to do?" Bartimaeus asked for his sight, and I blessed him with it. Beggars are at service stations asking for gas and on the street corners. When you encounter a beggar, do you go by the individual's dress and cleanliness, whether the individual is male or female, or the Spirit of God to determine if you will assist them? Do you hand them money or throw money out the window? No, the Bible does not state that I helped every beggar, nor will you. If you listen to the Holy Spirit in your decision-making process, the Holy Spirit will lead and guide you in what to give and to which beggar.

An aha moment: If you do not listen to and follow the Holy Spirit as a part of your daily spiritual activity, how do you expect to hear the Holy Spirit when you encounter a beggar or other situations? The Holy Spirit is your best guidance counselor. "Then they came to Jericho. As Jesus and his disciples, together with a large crowd, were leaving the city, a blind Bartimaeus, the son of Timaeus, was sitting by the roadside begging." Mark 10:46 (NIV) *Peace and blessings.*

Peace And Blessings : with the Risen *SON*

Day
One Hundred and Fifty Four

Believe in God

Making a change! I am sharing this as a reminder of what
I have in store for you. Do not be troubled by the sins and
immoral acts in this world. In times like these, as disciples,
you must remain faithful, trusting, and exhibiting the fruit of
the Spirit because you are a "fisher of men." Receive God's
blessing and love. "Let not your heart be troubled: ye believe
in God and me. In my Father's house are many mansions: if
it were not so, I would have told you. I am going to prepare a
place for you. And if I go and prepare a place for you, I will
come again, and receive you unto myself; where I am, there
ye may be also. And whither I go ye know, and the way ye
know. Thomas saith unto him, Lord, we know not whither
thou goest; how can we know the way? I saith unto him,
I am the way, the truth, and the life: no man cometh unto
the Father but by me. If ye had known me, ye should have
known my Father also: and from henceforth ye know him,
and have seen him." John 14:1- 7 (KJV)
Peace and blessings.

Peace And Blessings : with the Risen *SON*

Day
One Hundred and Fifty Five

A Clean Temple

The Holy Spirit resides in your body, also known as the temple. The Holy Spirit does not stay in an unclean temple because of its misuse. Ask Me to purify your temple daily or hourly if required so you can enjoy the presence of the Holy Spirit. As disciples, you belong to God, who sacrificed Me, His Son, for your salvation. Let Me clean your temple from the inside out to push the impurities out of you so that you can breathe fresh spiritual air. Lord, move in me today; my soul desires to let your Spirit have its way. Touch Me, Lord, and I will never be the same. Amen. "What? Know not that your body is the temple of the Holy Ghost, which is in you, which ye have of God, and you are not your own? For ye are bought with a price: therefore, glorify God in your body, and in your spirit, which is God's." 1 Corinthians 6:19-20 *Peace and blessings.*

Peace And Blessings : with the Risen *SON*

Day
One Hundred and Fifty Six

What is Your Worth?

Have you ever considered your value? Worth should be considered two-fold: one of the values you leave behind in terms of houses, money, and your legacy when you are dead, and second, the value or your worth when living. If you have assets to leave others when you are dead, then you are valuable to them more dead than alive. At the same time, I find you more valuable alive than dead. For Me, you are more useful alive than dead because of your witnessing to others, because, after death comes My judgment. Because of your living value and effectiveness, Satan is more interested in your death because you are destroying his plan. While living, I gave you the mission of spreading the gospel, which means your living will not be in vain.

When considering your worth, how many lives are attached to your living worth? How many lives are changed because of the daily life you display of Me being your Lord and Savior? How many lives are changed when they see you showing the fruit of the spirit and Me blessing you daily? Is your life worth living? Yes, because you are worth more alive than dead. My death makes your value "PRICELESS."
Peace and blessings.

Peace And Blessings : with the Risen *SON*

Day
One Hundred and Fifty Seven

Bragging Rights

"A person plans his course, but the LORD directs his steps."
Proverbs 16:9 (NET)

Daily you plan what you want to accomplish. Some days you are successful and other days you move items to the next day. It is said that the best-laid plans of mice and men will fail, especially if God is not involved. When God directs your steps there is much more that takes place. God has plans for you, therefore, He is arranging, organizing, and preparing things for your arrival. When you are a disciple of mine (Jesus), your pace, your movement, your words, your actions, your deeds, and your thoughts are directed by God. Do not deviate from the course or path. Do not try to accelerate the outcome.

Don't try to make things happen because you are impatient. If God needed your assistance He would tell you. Be patient and your blessing will be waiting for you. Allow God to order your steps and watch how things fall into place for you on your journey. ***Peace and blessings.***

Peace And Blessings : with the Risen *SON*

Day
One Hundred and Fifty Eight

The Potter

The potter represents Me, who takes clay and makes various vessels to sell. If I identify a fault during molding, I rework the clay into a better piece. As disciples, you must come to Me daily to be reworked because you are sinners saved by grace. Here is the beauty of this message: you can come to Me and tell Me you are all jacked up and to fix you. And I will fix you up from the inside out; that's how clay is shaped. When you enter a relationship with Me, you enter dirty and broken, but I will clean and heal you as only I can. I am patiently waiting for you! I cannot wait to reshape and mold you into a better Christian. After your reformation, do not forget to thank and Praise Me for making you a better person. "So I went down to the potter's house, where he was, working at his wheel. And the vessel he was making of clay was spoiled in the potter's hand, and he reworked it into another vessel, as it seemed good to the potter to do." Jeremiah 18:3 (CSB) *Peace and blessings.*

Day
One Hundred and Fifty Nine

The Potter's Fire

I heal, fix, mold, and reshape those who yield to My will. Once I rework you, I place you in the furnace to put the finishing touch on you. I build a fire in the stove, and after the furnace reaches a specific temperature, it is time to experience the fire. I take you through the fire, not around it, because you learn, develop, and mature by going through it. This process causes you to gain wisdom and become a stronger Christian. You are the salt of the earth.

When you face adversity (fire), let Me take you through it and get your blessings when you arrive on the other side. Shadrach, Meshach, and Abednego made it through and were blessed. ***Peace and blessings.***

Peace And Blessings : with the Risen *SON*

Day
One Hundred and Sixty

Be Anxious for Nothing!

Your goal is to be led by Me; therefore, you must
be relaxed to make things happen because things are
slower than you desire. Your timetable is different
from Mine. You must spend your time praying and
thanksgiving with Me while I put things in place for
you. Time spent in prayer with Me enhances your
relationship with Me. If you cannot wait for Me this
year, you have yet to grow, learn, or mature from where
you were last year. Be anxious for nothing this year.
Have faith and trust Me in all things. Do not be anxious
about anything. Instead, in every situation, through
prayer and petition with thanksgiving, tell your requests
to God." Philippians 4:6 (NET) *Peace and blessings.*

Day
One Hundred and Sixty One

Be Anxious (Part II)

When you are anxious and decide to make things happen because they are not working out as fast as you want, you interrupt My plan. I have all the knowledge and power, and everything is being put in place to make you successful. You apply for a job, but I know who needs to be on the interview board to get you hired. But your anxiousness ruined My plan, and you did not get the job. I directed you to a car dealership, but you decided to go to another dealership for the same type and style of car. The dealer added everything to increase his profit. My dealer was prepared to reduce or give you these items for free. Do not be the anxious person you were last week, month, or year. Being worried and making things happen is one powerful statement to Me. Do not let your actions make this statement this year!
Peace and blessings.

Peace And Blessings : with the Risen *SON*

Day
One Hundred and Sixty Two

A Subtle Enemy

Synonyms for subtle are cunning, deceitful, treacherous, wily, crafty, skillful, clever, or more ingenious. The serpent was more subtle than all the other creatures I made. The serpent placed a thought in Eve's mind to ponder, "What did Adam tell her that I said." That is the way Satan works on humankind, using a play of words better known as heresy (false information). As disciples of Mine, know your enemy and their ability to manipulate your mind. Satan wants to remind you of "the good old days" when you enjoyed the pleasures of your old self and your dark past. Satan knows your strengths and weaknesses and wants you to partner with him in sin. But when you walk with Me, I will show you the enemy's plan so you can avoid the trap. " Now the serpent was more subtle than any beast of the field which the LORD God had made. And he said unto the woman, Yea, hath God said, Ye shall not eat of every tree of the garden? "Genesis 3:1 (KJV) Walk in My Light. *Peace and blessings.*

Day *One Hundred and Sixty Three*

Chosen by God

Satan has come before Me after going to and fro in all the Earth. I challenged Him to try My servant, Job. He killed all of Job's livestock, his sons, and his daughters. And then Satan attacked Job's body. I chose you to represent Me as I have chosen Job. Could you endure the suffering? More importantly, can I select you as My upright servant as I did Job? As you go through things, realize that you are My disciple who was chosen to fight a spiritual battle.

Remember, as My servant, I limit what Satan can do to My chosen people. Job held on and was blessed with more than he initially had. Can you go through hardship and suffering and still receive your blessings? "And Satan answered the LORD, and said, Skin for skin, yea, all that a man hath will he give for his life. But put forth thine hand now, and touch his bone and his flesh, and he will curse thee to thy face. And the LORD said unto Satan, Behold, he is in thine hand, but save his life. "Job 2:4 (KJV) *Peace and blessings.*

Peace And Blessings : with the Risen *SON*

Day
One Hundred and Sixty Four

A Reprobate Mind

A reprobate mind is "a depraved, unprincipled, wicked individual who has been rejected by me and is beyond the hope of salvation." The people of Sodom and Gomorrah were rebellious, and I consumed them by fire. Do you know Me, listen to My voice, and follow My guidance?

Do you know of anyone who does things that are not acceptable? In my eyes, that would be all of humanity. You are My disciple. Come closer to Me, and you will learn to sin less and less every day. Learn from Me. Turn from your wicked and sinful ways, and I will not reject you. "And just as they did not see fit to acknowledge God any longer, God gave them over to a depraved mind, to do those things which are not proper. "Romans 1:28 (NASB) *Peace and blessings.*

Day
One Hundred and Sixty Five

Identification through Baptism!

I sacrificed My life as a ransom for your sin. Since you have accepted My sacrifice through baptism, you should walk in the newness of life. Just as God the Father raised Me from death to life, walking in the newness of life displays the death of your former sinful living. Sinfulness is extra baggage. It slows down your progression to Christian living. When you accept Me, you drop the baggage and can move freely because the ball and chain of sin are broken. What I have set free is free indeed. I have given you a new identity. You must continuously walk in the light I have provided for you. "Therefore we were buried with Him through baptism into death, that just as Christ was raised from the dead by the glory of the Father, even so we also should walk in newness of life." Romans 6:4 (KJV)
Peace and blessings.

Peace And Blessings : with the Risen *SON*

Day
One Hundred and Sixty Six

Can You Surrender?

All to Jesus, I surrender; All to Him I freely give; I will ever love and trust Him, In His presence daily live. One of the most challenging events, situations, or stages in a person's life is to give up control. As you know, there are a lot of control freaks in society. For some individuals, to give up power is a death sentence. Take this test, give up your cell phone for a day, and watch as you and others go crazy. That is the effect of having and being in control. You must surrender to Me so I can get the most out of your time and talents. To make this even more challenging, I am erasing the word surrender and changing it to submit to Him. Can you submit, accept, or yield to Me a superior force of authority? If you cannot surrender to a person you can see, how will you surrender to Me, whom you do not physically see??
Peace and blessings.

Day
One Hundred and Sixty Seven

Counting the Cost

At a gas station, someone approached several individuals asking for money to complete a journey. That individual did not count the cost before starting his journey. He was not ashamed to ask for money. This was how he planned his journeys regularly. I make known to My disciples what it will cost to follow Me. Have you considered what it will cost you to become a disciple of Mine?

Are you willing to lay it all down and follow Me? The more you love your actions, the greater the penalty will be. Becoming my disciple is far greater than what you are leaving behind. What are you willing to give up to become more like me? "For which of you, intending to build a tower, sitteth not down first, and counteth the cost, whether he have sufficient to finish it? Luke 14:28 (KJV) *Peace and blessings.*

Peace And Blessings : with the Risen *SON*

Day
One Hundred and Sixty Eight

Metamorphosis

"And be not conformed to this world: but be ye transformed
by the renewing of your mind, that ye may prove what
that good, and acceptable, and perfect, will of God is."
Romans 12:2 (KJV) A worm-like caterpillar crawls on the
ground, eating plants. After some time, it builds a cocoon
around itself and will emerge later as a beautiful butterfly.
One definition of metamorphosis is the transformation
of an immature form to a mature form. The caterpillar's
transformation brought forth a renewed creature, now a
beautiful butterfly. Consider your transformation when you
accept Me as your Savior and what you become. Are you
a new creature that has not conformed to this world? Your
metamorphosis is the renewing of your mind to that which is
good, acceptable, and the perfect will of Mine.

The change brings forth maturity of the mind in the adult
form, no longer requiring milk, but now you can eat food
from the table of and with Me. You have put away your
childish thoughts and actions and are doing what pleases
Me rather than humanity. Metamorphosis transforms an
immature, sinful person into a mature disciple of Mine.
Peace and blessings.

Peace And Blessings : with the Risen *SON*

Day
One Hundred and Sixty Nine

Walk in the Light

When you connect with Me, your desire must be to please Me by doing things correctly. I will shine a light on your path and lead you to your destination. I AM challenging you to walk and conduct business in the light, in the open, above board, so no assumptions are made. Some individuals are day people, while others are night people.

Some people conduct their evil deeds behind closed doors. I need to inform everyone there is no difference because I see in darkness as if it is daytime. Nevertheless, these individuals will be exposed. Therefore, hold my hand when challenges come and let us walk together. I will not leave nor forsake you. "Everyone who does evil hates the light and will not come into the light for fear that their deeds will be exposed." John 3:20 (KJV) *Peace and blessings.*

Peace And Blessings : with the Risen *SON*

Day
One Hundred and Seventy

An Aha Moment

He fell to the ground and heard a voice saying to him, "Saul, Saul, why are you persecuting me?" Acts 9:4 (NET) " Saul mistreated Christians because of their religious beliefs. He captured them and took them to Jerusalem for punishment or jail. As Saul approached Damascus, a light from heaven flashed around him, and he heard My voice say, "Saul, Saul, why are you persecuting Me?" My Light blinded Saul, and he heard My voice. The other men heard My voice but did not see anyone. What an Aha moment. Saul repented and became a Christian. Are you, like Saul, doing all the wrong things? If you are living a life like Saul, ask, and I will give you a chance to repent, change, and live a Christ-like life. I, Jesus, will forgive your mess. Like Saul, whose name was changed to Paul, you must change when I give you an aha moment. Hold my hand and walk with Me to lead you to righteousness.

Peace and blessings.

Day One Hundred and Seventy One

Walk with Me

When you walk with other individuals, do you walk beside, in front, or behind them? The optimum phrase is "walk with." Have you ever looked at how you walk with Me? Do you walk before me because My actions are too slow for your timetable? When you are in front of Me, you have already passed the things I have prepared for you because now they are behind you. Are you a sheep?

Sheep follow their Shepherd because sheep know their Shepherd's voice. A shepherd prods goats along because they run all over the area. Will you walk with Me and follow Me along your journey? I created time, weather, people, light, the universe, and everything else. When I return, walk with and follow me so you will stay caught up. "My sheep listen to my voice; I know them, and they follow me. John 10: 27 (NLT) *Peace and blessings.*

Peace And Blessings : with the Risen *SON*

Day
One Hundred and Seventy Two

None like Me

"To whom can you compare and liken me? Tell me whom you think I resemble so we can be compared!" Isaiah 46:5 (NET)

There is none like me. There is only one God. Images are built of heavy wood, iron, and metal that animals cannot pull. These false gods have no life and are made by man. I am the great I Am, the creator of man who wants to be greater than me. Look around, search your neighborhood, city, state, nation, and even travel to other countries, and you will not find anything or anyone to compare me with. There is none like me. I am the true living God. I announced the end from the beginning.

I am the alpha and omega. Remember what I accomplished in antiquity (the pass)! Truly, I am God; I have no peer; I am God, and there is none like me. Lift holy hands and praise me, humble your hearts and adore me, open your spirit and recognize me for who I Am, because none can challenge me, be like me or be compared to or with me. I will not leave or forsake you in your time of need; call on me, and I will be there because I am already there. Praise and honor me, the great I AM. *Peace and blessings.*

Peace And Blessings : with the Risen *SON*

Day
One Hundred and Seventy Three

In His Rest

When you rest, you relax and choose not to engage in tedious activities. NLT) Hebrews 4:1. "God's promise of entering his rest still stands, so we ought to tremble with fear that some of you might fail to experience it." "I left you a promise of entering into My rest; that is, of entering into a covenant-relation with Me and a state of communion with God through Me. You can enter that rest by faith.

Five features of this rest for the believer:
1) Rest means peace with God. 2) Rest means freedom in the worship and service of God. 3) Rest means deliverance from the burden of Mosaic observance (laws of Moses). 4) Rest means the freedom of worship according to the gospel. 5) Rest means the rest that God Himself enjoys." (Blue Letter Bible Commentary)

To enter My rest is like being in My presence with no worries, no concerns, no cares other than just being with Me. Adjust your calendar or schedule, enter your sacred space, and find rest in Me. *Peace and blessings.*

Peace And Blessings : with the Risen *SON*

Day
One Hundred and Seventy Four

Spoken Word

"But no human being can tame the tongue. It is a restless evil, full of deadly poison." James 3:8 (NIV)

A pastor was assigned to a woman known for her sin of spreading gossip. He instructed her to take a feather pillow to the top of the church bell tower, rip it open, and let the wind blow all the feathers away. He told her to come down from the bell tower and collect all the feathers scattered throughout the town. The poor lady, of course, could not do it — and that was the point that underscored the destructive nature of her gossip. Words continue to dishonor and divide many days, months, and years after they are spoken, and they linger in people's minds and pass from one talebearer to the next. You must be careful of the words you speak. Words are quickly spoken but challenging to retract. Could you gather all the false statements you made, whether by mistake or purposefully? Be careful of what you say because whiteout does not erase spoken words. Hold my hand, listen to my voice, and love others unconditionally despite their faults. By the way, you have faults also. ***Peace and blessings.***

Day
One Hundred and Seventy Five

Life and Death In The Tongue

"The tongue has the power of life and death, and those who love it will eat its fruit." Proverbs 18:21 (NIV)

James says no one can tame the tongue. When evil comes from your mouth, three individuals are slain: the slanderer, the slandered, and the listener. The slanderer is the person making false statements; the slandered is the person the statements are about; the listener is the person hearing the information. He who guards his mouth and tongue keeps his soul from distress. When words are many, sin is unavoidable, but he who restrains his lips is wise. Change your thought process. Tell the world the good news of my coming from heaven, walking on water, raising the dead, healing the sick, and dying on the cross. Be a witness of your salvation and physical healing. If you take the time to talk about me, you should not have time to talk about others. When you talk about me, you are speaking life to others.
Peace and blessings.

Peace And Blessings : with the Risen *SON*

Day
One Hundred and Seventy Six

Living Versus Existing

"Again Jesus spoke to them, saying, "I am the light
of the world. Whoever follows me will not walk in
darkness but will have the light of life."
John 8:12 (ESV)

Kathy Bates from the movie The Family that Prey
asked her friend a question; "Are you living, or are you
just existing?" To exist is to live at a minimal level.
At the same time, living means having a life rich in
experience. Which are you doing? When you walk in
My Light, your life changes. With Me, you experience
walking in love, your joy is enhanced, and you find
peace beyond human understanding. Your faith in Me
will then cause your cup to overflow. Your life is filled
with My light, and you are no longer surrounded by
darkness. Allow Me to live in you and you in Me, and
you can experience real living beyond existing. Walk
with Me and enjoy living in and with the light.
Peace and blessings.

Peace And Blessings : with the Risen *SON*

Day
One Hundred and Seventy Seven

Daylight Savings Time

In the spring, you move time forward by one hour; in the fall, you move time backward by one hour. You do this to get more daylight to work or play. You have no power to control time. I have the power to control time. Joshua asked for more daylight to win a battle. So, the sun stood still, and the moon stopped, till the nation avenged itself of its enemies, as it is written in the Book of Jashar. The sun stopped in the middle of the sky and delayed going down about a full day (Joshua 10:13) KJV). Now that was time management, where a 24-hour day became a 48-hour day. I control time from the cradle to the grave or from beginning to end. That is the power of the God you serve. Your definition of time is the space between one event and another. You must remember I control time. You must manage it wisely. Take advantage of every day, hour, minute, and second. You never know when it is your last or when I will return. ***Peace and blessings.***

Peace And Blessings : with the Risen *SON*

Day
One Hundred and Seventy Eight

Can You Follow Me?

As I made my journey to the cross, I met many individuals. One was the gentleman who asked what he must do to inherit eternal life. It was a good question, but I knew he could not follow through, but I gave him the answer. I told him to sell what he had and give it to people experiencing poverty, then come and follow me. He hung his head down and walked away. People ask questions but are not ready for the answers. If I gave you this same answer, could you or are you willing to let go of all you have acquired and follow me? You may say yes because you know I'm in heaven. If you are listening to the Holy Spirit, you may be directed to do something unbelievable and challenging. Can you follow me, or are you willing to follow me? Foxes have holes, birds have a nest, but the son of man has nowhere to lay his head. If you follow me, My Father will bless you with an everlasting journey in His kingdom. Are you willing to follow me? *Peace and blessings.*

Day
One Hundred and Seventy Nine

Your Actions Speak Louder Than Words

Titus 1:16: "They claim to know God, but they deny him by their works. I told My disciples, "If you love me, keep my commandments." Your actions and deeds must match your words. You must mean what you say and say what you mean. Living a double standard makes you like the Pharisees, Sadducees, and Scribes I discussed. My Father will send Me back to a church without a spot or wrinkle. No one knows the day or hour of my return, including me. Stop sneaking around sinning because those around you and the US (Father, Son, and the Holy Spirit) already know what you are doing and who is involved with you.

Stop acting like there is no God; change your lifestyle for the better so you can go to heaven with Me when I return. I have more to offer you than what you will leave behind. Your actions are a positive or negative sermon for others to see. Your actions are seen and speak louder than your words. ***Peace and blessings.***

Peace And Blessings : with the Risen *SON*

Gratitude

Day
One Hundred and Eighty

Your Influence

Romans 13:21 Do not be overcome by evil but overcome evil with good." Let's define the word influence. Influence is the capacity to affect character, development, or behavior. Who influenced you to be who you are today? Who do you influence? How do you use your influence to motivate people? Influence can be positive or negative. It can come from your presence, actions, words, and deeds. Those around you may be watching and imitating what they see you doing. I influenced some of My disciples with this statement; "Come ye after me, and I will make you become fishers of men." I Influence them to seek My kingdom. Influence them to stand still and pray. Influence them to trust Me with all their heart and lean not unto their understanding. Influence them to follow the guidance of the Holy Spirit, and My Father will bless them. Praise them for being examples to those under their influence as you were to them. ***Peace and blessings.***

Day
One Hundred and Eighty One

Your Word is Your Bond

It has been stated that a man's word is his bond. There are many definitions of the word bond. In my discussion, a bond is an agreement. Growing up, your father may have agreed with another person, and no document was signed. Your father's word that he would do something was the contract. My father made a bond or promise to Abraham, Isaac and Jacob. If My Father said it, He meant it. He does not lie, and His words are actual. Have you made promises that you knew were difficult to keep? People hold Christians to their word and do not accept you're making a mistake or unknowingly being wrong. I told you I would never leave or forsake you, and I was there for you. My words are my bond. ***Peace and blessings.***

Day
One Hundred and Eighty Two

Looking Beyond Your Nose

Much of your anger and wrath comes from being self- centered and not others-centered. When you take yourself out of the picture or look beyond your nose, you will see others, not yourself. Be slow to speak to avoid saying words that cannot be taken back. During the recent gas shortage, you witnessed self-centered individuals buying extra gas to fill various containers. If you treat others how you want to be treated, you will focus on helping others first. I will not leave or forsake you because I am your Shepherd; control your anger so you can be all I desire and complete the task I have given you. My dear brothers and sisters, take note of this: Everyone should be quick to listen, slow to speak, and slow to become angry because human anger does not produce the righteousness that I desire." James 1:19-20 (NIV) *Peace and blessings.*

Day
One Hundred and Eighty Three

Amen

I want you to utter Amen at the end of a prayer or hymn because it means 'so be it" and is also used to express agreement or approval. Amen is used 24 times in the Old Testament. Amen is a New Testament word used 52 times in the Synoptic Gospels—Matthew, Mark, and Luke—and 25 times in the gospel. The total number of times it is used in the New Testament is 129. According to your translation, the number of amens in the Bible increases or decreases. You may use other words like amen. Let me use other similar words, such as indeed, yes, so be it, okay, exactly, most assuredly, absolutely, correct affirmative, indeed, as you say, or yep. After the doxology, the song after prayer, you usually sing amen. I am sharing the word amen so you will know what you are saying and how you may be saying it. If you agree with Me being your Lord and Savior, say Amen.
Peace and blessings.

Peace And Blessings : with the Risen *SON*

Day
One Hundred and Eighty Four

A Powerful God

"And God said, Let there be light: and there was light."
Genesis 1:3 (KJV) There are many bible translations of
the Bible. Most of the translations are word for word
regarding verse three. Notice the simplicity of the
wording and the action that followed. I am sharing with
you the power of speaking. I speak, and things happen.
Let me help you out of your box. You call on Me and
look for Me to show up, and all I must do is speak from
My location (which is everywhere) and answer your
request. I healed the Syrophoenician Woman's Daughter
(Matthew 15:21-28), the Centurion's Servant (Matthew
8:5-13), and the Capernaum Official's Son (John 4:46-
54) from another location. I spoke of healing, which
took place from where I was. Release Me from (figure
of speech) the area or place because you limit what I
can do for you. *Peace and blessings.*

Day One Hundred and Eighty Five

The Words of My Mouth

Every day, you speak words from your mouth, which come from the heart. Some are pleasant, and others are outright rude, but they come from your heart. To have a clean mouth, you need a clean heart. Your heart is the core of your thought process. It is what you put in your heart that comes from your mouth. Good input, sound output. Sinful input, sinful output. Once words exit your mouth, they cannot be captured or taken back. Take time to read and study the Bible to train your heart before your mouth speaks. Meditate with Me to empty yourself of the evil lurking within. Read and study the Bible, learn of Me, and watch your heart and words change. Then, the words in your mouth will become acceptable in my sight as you know My language.

"For we all stumble in many ways. If someone does not stumble in what he says, he is a perfect individual, able to control the entire body." James 3:2. "Let the words of my mouth, and the meditation of my heart, be acceptable in thy sight, O Lord my strength, and my redeemer." Psalms 19:14 (KJV) *Peace and blessings.*

Peace And Blessings : with the Risen *SON*

Day *One Hundred and Eighty Six*

Don't Forget to Praise God

While passing through Samaria and Galilee, I met ten men with leprosy. Leprosy is a contagious disease that affects the skin. Individuals with leprosy had to stay away from people so the disease would not spread. They called on Me to heal them. Having compassion, I told them to show themselves to the priest. As they went along, they were healed. The healing came in their faith in Me and following the instructions they received. I sent them to the priest to be inspected so they could re-enter society. Their nationality is not given, but only one returned to give thanks, and he was a Samaritan. The one despised, not liked, shunned, hated by the Jews, and so much more was the only one to return and praise the Lord. The ten asked for healing, but nine did not return praises.

Are you among the nine or the Samaritan in your attendance and praise? You called me for healing, and I answered your call, but most of you failed to send praises. Praise Me from whom all your blessings come, and more will follow. Can I hear hallelujah from the one who came back? "And one of them, when he saw that he was healed, returned, and with a loud voice glorified God." Luke 17:15 (NET)
Peace and blessings.

Peace And Blessings : with the Risen *SON*

Day One Hundred and Eighty Seven

It is Seasoned with Salt

Have you ever listened to someone answer a person's questions without concern for the tone or harsh words? Speaking with harsh words is nothing new; even in Paul's era, society used harsh words when talking to each other. Grace is a way of moving that is smooth and attractive. Our speech should be smooth or soft. The beautiful part is that it is accessible to the ears, which causes a person to hear and understand what is being said. Salt is the seasoning or the truth that must be told. Paul is saying that there is a way to make your point using salt but in a way that you are heard and do not become a roadblock or barrier to others finding or getting closer to Me. Are you aware of the tone and use of salt when responding to others? Softly and tenderly. "Let your speech be always with grace, seasoned with salt, that ye may know how ye ought to answer each one." Colossians 4:6 (KJV)
Peace and blessings.

Peace And Blessings : with the Risen *SON*

Day
One Hundred and Eighty Eight

Word On the Street

Some say John the Baptist; others say Elijah; and others say Jeremiah or one of the prophets. These are the answers I received when I asked who men say I am. The word on the street can precede you before you arrive and exceed you by giving you more credit for things you didn't do. Do not chase rumors or the word on the street. More is added to enhance the story as information is passed from one person to another. Even as I traveled in and around Jerusalem, there was lots of added information about the miracles I did, the people I talked to, and the friends I visited. Be sure you speak only of truthful information. Rumors break relationships and cause chaos and confusion. We, Father, Son, and the Holy Spirit, are not the authors of confusion. As a Christian, you should not be the author of confusion. Speak the truth and leave the unknown alone; do not assume. ***Peace and blessings.***

Peace And Blessings : with the Risen *SON*

Day
One Hundred and Eighty Nine

Paul Harvey

Have you ever incurred a false witness? Someone who tells the inaccurate truth, which makes them look good. When I was growing up, a commentator named Paul Harvey would take any story and research it. He would tell what everyone already knew, and when he finished recalling what everyone knew, he would say, "And now the rest of the story." He would tell all the unknowns that were not told, and the public learned the actual details, and a false witness was discovered. Every story has a second side when it deals with people. When we take one side, we are vulnerable to a false witness. Our culture and understanding of words make us see and understand things differently. You should get all the details and remind others that any story has two sides. "False witnesses did rise; they laid to my charge things that I knew not." Psalms 35:13 (KJV)
Peace and blessings.

 Peace And Blessings : with the Risen *SON*

Day One Hundred and Ninety

The Power of a Word

Here, we have one unworthy of Me to come under his roof to heal one of his servants. One that is unworthy but full of faith, maybe more than some Christians. Did you catch that? Without faith, it is impossible to please God. Even unworthy from the centurion's perspective, his faith got My attention, and I healed his servant. The centurion asked Me to say that his servant might be healed. I healed his servant. The power of words is more significant than you realize. "Lord," the centurion replied, "I am not worthy to have You come under my roof. But only say the word, and my servant will be cured." Matthew 8:8 (KJV) As disciples, watch what you say because your words become life. Check out John 6:63; you have more power than you realize.

Peace and blessings.

Day
One Hundred and Ninety One

Forgiveness Frees the Soul

Let me share words from "Grace for the Moment" by Max Lucado. Is there any emotion imprisons the soul more than the unwillingness to forgive? What do you do when people mistreat you or those you love? Does the fire of anger boil within you, with leaping flames consuming your emotion? Or do you reach somewhere, to some source of cool water, and pull out a bucket of mercy to free yourself? Don't get on the roller coaster of resentment and anger. Be the one who says, "Yes, he mistreated me, but I will be like Christ. Be the one who says, "Forgive them, Father, they don't know what they are doing. Be the one who declares I am walking with My Savior! "If you suffer for doing good, and you are patient, then God is pleased—(I Peter 2:20). *Peace and blessings.*

Peace And Blessings : with the Risen *SON*

Day
One Hundred and Ninety Two

Improper Conversations

Paul encourages the Ephesians to avoid obscene conversations, foolish talking that lacks good sense, or telling coarse or unthoughtful jokes. Even today, on your jobs, some individuals gather around the coffee pot telling off-color jokes, rude comments about women, or making sexual double-entendres. It is up to you to speak up against these conversations. If you do not speak up, you tell the individual that you accept this conversation.
James reminds us of the importance of controlling our tongues. Once spoken, you cannot take back your words; therefore, it may be better to be quiet. More and more public individuals are brought forward because of comments made to people privately or publicly. Don't do what others do just to fit in. You can control what you hear. If you don't, you may lose your inheritance and home in heaven with Me, Jesus.

"Obscene stories, foolish talk, and coarse jokes–these are not for you. Instead, let there be thankfulness to God. Ephesians 5:4 (NLT):" If you find yourself in moments where this is a challenge, ask Me to help you control your conversation.
Peace and blessings.

Peace And Blessings : with the Risen *SON*

Day
One Hundred and Ninety Three

Imprint

When born, ducklings accept the first animal or person they see as their parent. The mother duck is always close when they hatch to ensure they identify her. When a baby is born, the nurse connects the baby to its mother whose heartbeat it has heard in her womb. In Christianity, the new member often recognizes the person in the church who shared the "Good News" when they accepted Me as their Savior. Are you spreading the gospel? That is why you were created. Have you gained their trust? Are they looking to you for additional guidance as they mature?

Salvation occurs when you evangelize and spread the "gospel.'" Maybe you have been busy just doing what you want, or you may have been spreading gossip, but that is not why I created you. Make it your mission to praise and worship Me. Spread the "Good News" about Me. Go into all the world and proclaim the gospel to the whole creation. I accepted you and guided you. Do as I have done. If you decide not to, I, Jesus, will find others who are willing and bless them. ***Peace and blessings.***

Peace And Blessings : with the Risen *SON*

Day
One Hundred and Ninety Four

Gratitude

Gratitude is the state of being grateful or thankful.

Gratitude is a thankful appreciation for what an individual receives, whether tangible (touchable) or intangible (untouchable). Some individuals are thankful for the slightest thing you do for them. They thank and praise you repeatedly. Then, some are never grateful, as if you are supposed to do things for them anyway. Now that you see both ends of the spectrum, which one are you when it comes to praising God? Are you grateful, or do you think and believe I am supposed to do things for you regardless? *Peace and blessings.*

Day
One Hundred and Ninety Five

Praise Me

Nevertheless, on how you feel, "Praise Me from whom all blessings flow. Praise Me all creatures here below." You were created to praise God the Father. Be grateful for the blessings you receive even if you did not ask for them. Do not let the rocks praise Me just because you do not. Show gratitude in the morning, at noon, and the closing of another day. When praises go up, blessings come down. Do not worry; many falling blessings do not hit non-praisers. ***Peace and blessings.***

Day
One Hundred and Ninety Six

Praise, Praise, And More Praise

Psalms 100 (KJV): "Make a joyful noise unto the LORD, all ye lands. Serve the LORD with gladness: come before his presence with singing. I enjoy hearing your praises.

It is a joyful noise in my ear. Your praises make Me feel appreciated, as you feel the same way when others praise you. The book of Psalms shares lots of praises from King David. You do know that if you do not praise me the rocks will cry out praises. Surely you do not want a rock to praise Me just because you were ashamed to praise Me before Man. Slow down, think about all the beautiful things I have done in your life, and let your praises go up, and my blessings will come down. *Peace and blessings.*

Day
One Hundred and Ninety Seven

Are You Thankful?

"Giving thanks always for all things unto God and the Father in the name of our Lord Jesus Christ;" Ephesians 5:20 (KJV)

Have you ever considered your blessings? Maybe you are not knowledgeable of your blessings. You were awakened this morning, but it didn't just happen. You have shelter, food, and warmth, and you are loved. Do you consider that regardless of your health, you are blessed? You may have pain, but you are still enjoying this journey called life. Are you working, even if it may not be your dream job? Paul says to give thanks for all things. The more you thank Me, regardless of whether you believe it to be good or bad, the more I bless us. Thank Me for the rain and the sunshine days. Some suffer from sinusitis but thank Me for the pollen because it starts the process of a beautiful green spring and summer. Thank Me for the snow and cold weather; the cold kills the germs, and snow cleans the air. The vehicle you are driving is better than what others may have. The reality is, the more you are thankful for what you have and are going through, your being thankful encourages Me to bless you more and give you better conditions. As you grow closer to Me, your thankfulness should increase. *Peace and blessings.*

Peace And Blessings : with the Risen *SON*

Day
One Hundred and Ninety Eight

In Everything, Give Thanks

"In everything give thanks: for this is the will of God in Christ Jesus concerning you." I Thessalonians 5:18(KJV) Paul talks to the Thessalonians about being at peace with themselves. Being at peace, being content, being satisfied, or being happy are all ingredients to being thankful.

Today, praise Me! Thank Me for blessing you. Thank Me. There is so much to be thankful for. The pilgrims thanked God for food and shelter. The reality is that Thanksgiving is every day. I am your Creator and can take away blessings just as quickly. Be a recipient of My generosity and praise Me for all things. In everything, give thanks. Express your gratitude for My kindness, patience, protection, grace, and mercy. I love you despite all of your imperfections and provide your daily for your needs. *Peace and blessings.*

Day
One Hundred and Ninety Nine

Blessed Beyond Measure

"Now to him who is able to do immeasurably more than all we ask or imagine, according to his power that is at work within us." Ephesians 3:20 (NIV)

This is where the saying that you are "blessed beyond measure" comes from. The word measure is used to determine a unit of measure, like a length, a width, a height, a weight, or a space of time. What method of measuring can you use to measure My blessings? When I bless you, there is no measurable tool or process to determine the length, width, height, weight, or the time I used to bless you. What I do for My sheep is immeasurable beyond humanity's comprehension. I am "unfigure-outable." (Lol, new word) There's a song that says, "You can't beat My giving." There is so much truth to this song. I don't know about you, but "BLESS ME, GOD, BLESS ME." Do not try to measure your blessings, but be ever more thankful and praise Me for them. Enjoy My blessings. ***Peace and blessings.***

Peace And Blessings : with the Risen *SON*

Day
Two Hundred

Thank You

What is life without challenges, boring? Accept life challenges as they develop your wisdom and growth. Enhance your theological education or continuously read and study the Bible to learn of Me. When you stay in tune and focused on Me, you will gather much knowledge, and I will have much more to share with you. Thank Me daily for the information I give you to make you a better person. Each day, you must grow closer to me spiritually.

Depart with more excellent knowledge and understanding of Me. As you find your mission, walk closer with Me, and your challenges will become small pebbles and not mountains. Thank Me often, and your blessings will flow. ***Peace and blessings.***

Peace And Blessings : with the Risen *SON*

Your Season is
Changing!

Embrace and Prepare for the Change

A Season of Preservation

Look at My promises and how they preserved you. Remember, I have never lied. If I said it, I will do it. During this season, you will have many opportunities to shine a light on yourself! This is to bring awareness to overlooked things that could sabotage your growth in Me. During this season, you will be given things to consider, such as correcting your behavior and removing items hidden in your heart. Don't worry; everyone has something to throw out. Take advantage of the assistance of the Holy Spirit to deliver you through this season. The Holy Spirit comes alongside to guide you down the intended path for your life. Because I love you, I will chastise you to shape you into the person I predestined you to be; that's what parents do when they love their children. Love never fails.

During this season, you will explore the following sub-topics:

Gods Promises Bring Preservation

The Gift of Correction: Positive or Negative Love

Gods Promises Bring Preservation

Day
Two Hundred and One

Inheritance

Inheritance may be inherited property passing at the owner's death to the heir or those entitled to succeed; legacy; to take or receive property, a right, a title, etc., by succession or will as an heir. An inheritance is customarily given to a person after the death of a family member. The prodigal son asked for his portion (inheritance) before his Father died. I died on the cross for your sins. Individuals who accepted me as their Savior should inherit eternal life. Do not waste your inheritance as the prodigal son did. Esau sold his birthright to Jacob for a meal, not knowing what he had. Do not be enticed to give up your inheritance for something that appears better. What I am offering you cannot be matched by any human or Satan. The inheritance I have for you is for you. Listen to the Holy Spirit as he guides you on your life journey. My inheritance for you is a once-in-your-lifetime journey; take advantage of it. Your inheritance is waiting for you. *Peace and blessings.*

Day
Two Hundred and Two

Inheritance Pt. 2

Inheritance refers to the assets an individual bequeaths (leaves) to their loved ones after passing. Today, a person leaves a Will or a Trust with their wishes to distribute their assets. I left my heavenly home to restore a broken relationship with you and My Father. I was crucified (nailed on a cross) and died for humanity's sins. I rose on the third day and eventually returned to my heavenly home. I have an inheritance for those who accepted me as their Lord and Savior. What is in the inheritance I left for you? Revelation 21: And the twelve gates are pearls made from just one pearl! The main street of the city is pure gold, like transparent glass. The city does not need the sun or the moon to shine on it because the glory of God lights it up, and its lamp is the Lamb, Jesus. There is so much more, but this gives you an idea of what to expect. Come, get connected, or get closer to me so you can enjoy what My Father has in store for you. Prepare for the journey.

"Thanks to the Father, who has qualified you to share in the saints' inheritance in light. "Colossians 1:12 (ESV)
Peace and blessings.

Peace And Blessings : with the Risen *SON*

Day
Two Hundred and Three

Jesus Can Set You Free

Demons are evil/fallen angels who follow Satan instead of God. When Satan was cast out of heaven, the demons fell with him instead of staying in their place as God's ministers of good. They attack humans with Physical Illness, Mental Impairment, The Spread of False Doctrine, Spiritual Warfare, or Possession of a person. Do not give in to these demonic desires when dealing with depression, alzheimers, dementia, or suicidal thoughts.

Demon's mission is to make you feel alone and rejected by family, friends, and the church. But the Holy Spirit and I can cast out this evil spirit from you. In the Bible, the processed individuals came to Me for him to release them from this spirit. He will release this spirit from you if you ask in unwavering faith. Ask, and you shall receive. "Soon afterward, Jesus began a tour of the nearby towns and villages, preaching and announcing the Good News about the Kingdom of God. He took his twelve disciples and some women cured of evil spirits and diseases. Among them was Mary Magdalene, from whom he had cast out seven demons." Luke 8:1-2 (NLT) *Peace and blessings.*

Peace And Blessings : with the Risen *SON*

Day
Two Hundred and Four

Justification

Justification is the process by which sinners are made or declared righteous in the sight of God. "Being in such a sinful state, the only way you can be justified is to be justified freely. You can't purchase it with your good works at all. You can't have it if it isn't made accessible to you. So, you are justified freely by My grace — My unmerited favor, given to you without regard to what you deserve. It is motivated purely by the giver and by nothing in the one who receives. The harlot, the liar, the murderer, and the Christian all fall short because neither can touch the sky without Christ. It is through Jesus that you are justified or declared righteous in the sight of God. So don't think you are all that - without Christ, you are nothing. Justification is a gift given by Jesus Christ. "For all have sinned and fall short of the glory of God, and all are justified freely by his grace through the redemption that came by Christ Jesus." (NIV) Romans 3:23-24 *Peace and blessings.*

Peace And Blessings : with the Risen *SON*

Day
Two Hundred and Five

At Midnight

Some individuals begin their travel at this hour, and some go to work while others get off work. Midnight is considered the darkest hour of the night. Some call it the witching hour when evil's power is the strongest and black magic is the most powerful. Midnight is also a time of darkness in a person's life. Everyone endures a period of midnight, but how you deal with your midnight is a matter. Paul and Silas prayed, sang songs, and praised God; their morning came at midnight. They did not allow Satan to control their praise even in their midnight hour.

During your midnight hour, as disciples, do as Paul and Silas and praise God in the heat of your troubles, and God will show you the morning sun. It's something about "LIGHT" (JESUS) that brightens up a day. It's a beautiful blessing when God brings you through your troubles.

Pray, sing, and praise. "Weeping may tarry for the night, But joy cometh in the morning." Psalms 30:5 (ASV)
Peace and blessings.

Peace And Blessings : with the Risen *SON*

Day
Two Hundred and Six

See a Man

In this meeting, I was tired from My journey, and My disciples have gone to the city to get food. I am at a well dug by Jacob and requests water from a Samaritan woman. She questioned why a Jew would ask a Samaritan for water when Jews have no dealings with Samaritans. I offered her the living water so she would never thirst again. I asked her to bring her husband, and she did not have one. I told her she had five husbands, and the man with her now was not her husband. I told her I was the Messiah. She went into the city shouting, "Come see a man who knows all about me." I invite you to see a man who knows everything about you. I know your sinful nature, the desires of your heart, and your desire to receive salvation. I am your Savior, your Mediator who stands between you and God, who cleans your prayers and daily cleans your slate to present you faultless before God the Father. Meet a man named Jesus (His earthly name), then meet Christ (His heavenly name), who knows you and can save you. "Come, see a man who told me everything I ever did. Could this be the Messiah?" John 4:29 (NIV)

Peace and blessings.

Peace And Blessings : with the Risen *SON*

Day
Two Hundred and Seven

Chosen by God

Saul, one who persecuted the Christians, was chosen by God, who used his skills to locate and persecute Christians and was now chosen to locate Gentiles or the unsaved. What a tremendous change in mission. The catch is that people remembered Saul for what he used to be. It took time for his change to be accepted. Today, we are the same way. If a drug dealer or prostitute became a Christian, we continue to accept or judge them as to who they were, not who they have become. Saul, whose name was changed to Paul, had a challenging time becoming accepted. Do you judge every convert or just the ones named prostitute, drug dealer, homosexual, or pimp, and not have any concerns about the ones named thief, liars, or backbiter? Judging is wrong; therefore, you should not judge anyone. God chose Saul and turned his lousy behavior, and God can choose anyone and bring them from bad to good. Jesus died for all sinners, which included you when you were a fully engaged sinner.

Accept God's chosen "But the Lord said to him, "Go, for he is a chosen instrument of mine to carry my name before the Gentiles and kings and the children of Israel." Acts 9:15 (NIV) *Peace and blessings.*

Peace And Blessings : with the Risen *SON*

Day
Two Hundred and Eight

I Will Meet You in the Valley

In the valley of the shadow of death represents your darkest moments in life. Midnight is considered the darkest time of the night. Cancer, COVID-19, lung disease, foot pain, backache, sciatic nerve pain, and many other ailments can be your valley experience. Regardless of your fate, I, Jesus, will meet you in the valley and be your guiding light. In your darkness, I will be your light, your guide, your Comforter, as well as your Savior. Look upward in the valley if possible because you are already at your lowest. It only takes one candle to see the breaking of day, the breaking through your valley experience. Hold my hand as we walk together, and I will lead you out of the valley. "Yea, though I walk through the valley of the shadow of death," Psalms 23:4a (KJV). ***Peace and blessings.***

Day
Two Hundred and Nine

What is Peace?

Peace is freedom from disturbance or a period of tranquility. It is also a time of no war in the world or your family. That is humanity's definition of Peace. The Peace that I am offering you is beyond human understanding.

Peace is a period of quietness; Peace is a stillness of your thoughts; Peace is a stoppage of time to allow you to refresh, renew, and rebuild your resilience, or Peace is time spent with Me. Regardless of how you define or look at Peace, I can give it to you once you are attached to Me. When I give you Peace, you are neither afraid nor troubled. If you are ready to enjoy Peace, accept Me as your Lord and Savior, and your world of turmoil will fade away. "Peace I leave with you, my Peace I give unto you: not as the world giveth, give I unto you. Let not your heart be troubled, neither let it be afraid."
(KJV) John 14:27 *Peace and blessings.*

Peace And Blessings : with the Risen *SON*

Day
Two Hundred and Ten

That Glorious Day

All your life, you have heard that I, Jesus, is returning for My church. Every day, you see people going about their business and showing no concern for My return. That blessed and glorious day is closer than you would believe. I am just waiting for God the Father to tell me to return to His church. I do not know the day, hour, or second I will return, but I prepare. It will be a great day for some, so do not worry about what others are doing. You follow me and my commandments. Stay focused on Me and not the things of this world. You cannot take the things of this world into my kingdom. All I need in my kingdom is your soul. So that you can get there, hold my hand, and walk beside me for the rest of your journey. "Looking for that blessed hope, and the glorious appearing of the great God and our Saviour Jesus Christ;" Titus 2:13 (KJV) *Peace and blessings.*

Peace And Blessings : with the Risen *SON*

Day
Two Hundred and Eleven

Fear Not

Fear is "an unpleasant emotion caused by the belief that someone or something is dangerous, likely to cause pain or a threat." (Dictionary.com). No matter how brave a person appears, everyone has at least one fear. Today, society presents many things that cause fear, like COVID-19, gas shortages, cyber-attacks, job challenges, and much more. Fear is a factor in bringing or having control of individuals. Please do not allow these fears to affect your following me, your Savior. There is nothing new under the sun that I have made or controlled. Fear not because I am with you and will never forsake you. Fear not because I am your Shepherd and will take care of you. All you must do is trust and follow me. "Have I not commanded you? Be strong and courageous. Do not be afraid; do not be discouraged, for the LORD your God will be with you wherever you go." Joshua 1: 9 (NIV)
Peace and blessings.

Peace And Blessings : with the Risen *SON*

Day
Two Hundred and Twelve

Let Me Hold Something

Have you had friends who always ask for money whenever you see them? Let me hold something. You made a mistake one day and asked, "How much do you need, and how long do you need it?" Their response may be whatever you got, but the payback needs to be mentioned. They are beggars who are not located on typical corners. Peter and John saw this beggar daily as they went to the temple. He was always at the gate, called beautiful, asking for money. "Let me hold something." Peter said, "Fix your eyes on me. Silver and gold have I none, but I have to give thee such as in the name of Jesus Christ of Nazareth rise and walk." This beggar got more than he requested. Now he got up and could walk and get a job. Are we like beggars when we ask God for something since we always ask and seldom give back? Fix your eyes on Me so I can tell you, arise, and walk with Me by obeying My commandments.

If you walk with Me, your reward in heaven is more significant than what you receive on Earth. As Christians, ask your Shepherd, your Lord, and your Savior and Creator for your needs and desires. He is faithful in meeting all your needs as you communicate with Jesus and tell Him thank you. "And a confident man lame from his mother's womb was carried, whom they laid daily at the gate of the temple, which is called Beautiful, to ask alms of them that entered into the temple."

Acts 3:2 (KJV) *Peace and blessings.*

Peace And Blessings : with the Risen *SON*

Day
Two Hundred and Thirteen

Hope

"Hope is defined as to cherish a desire with anticipation: to want something to happen or be true." I feel what you are asking. Faith is complete confidence and trust in someone or something. Hope is a feeling of expectation and desire for something to happen. Individuals play the lottery hoping or anticipating winning the jackpot. Christians must have greater hope than winning the lottery. Your hope is built on nothing less than Jesus' blood and righteousness. I dare not trust the sweetest frame but wholly lean on Jesus' name. Other words for hope are anticipating, expecting, wishing, trusting, assuming, and always looking forward. You look forward to my return, which could be any day. Everybody is hoping for something positive to occur in their life. Walk with me and allow me to guide you to a blessed hope and desire to enter my kingdom. Continue reading your Bible to enhance your hope and faith. You believe, you hope, you trust, and the greater of these is faith, believing in the unseen with the assurance it will happen. You are my refuge and shield; I have put my hope in your word Psalms 119:114 (NIV). *Peace and blessings.*

Peace And Blessings : with the Risen *SON*

Day
Two Hundred and Fourteen

Don't Take God For Granted

You take things for granted by assuming things will always be the same. You lay down at night and get up the next day. There is no genuine concern about not waking up because it has been happening all your life. You used to go to church with praising Me in mind, but now you go to church. Habits can make you complacent or become self-satisfied. But when that head or tailwind comes and rocks your world, reality sets in, and like the Israelites, you return to Me. When September 11, 2001, occurred, America called on Me. The country has recovered, and "I AM" is no longer a part of America's need or acceptance even though your currency states, "In God, we trust." Where are you in this equation or common denominator of society? Step out of your comfort zone of complacency, do a reality check, ask Me for forgiveness, and rekindle your journey with Me. Allow Me to hold your hand this time so you will not slip. Walk beside me, and do not try to get ahead of Me. When you follow the leader, you follow. Allow Me to lead you down the path of righteousness so you can have the opportunity to enter my kingdom. When "I AM" in your life, you are centered.
Peace and blessings.

Peace And Blessings : with the Risen *SON*

Day
Two Hundred and Fifteen

What Is Your Stance?

Posture is the position in which someone holds their body when standing or sitting or a particular way of dealing with or considering something, an approach, or attitude.

When considering posture, you may think of how a person stands. Stand is used to represent a person's back or their decision. Mark 14:66-72 Peter took a posture, an approach, an attitude, or decided when challenged about knowing Me. When asked if he was one of My followers, he denied knowing Me out of weaknesses or fear. What is your posture or position about knowing Me in public? Matthew 10:33 (KJV) says, "But whosoever shall deny me before men, him will I also deny before my Father which is in heaven." Pray that you have the strength and courage to communicate, praise, and worship Me wherever you are. Take a stand, position, approach, take a stance, or decide to recognize Me as your Lord and Savior and publicly praise and honor Me. I realize You can approach, take a stance, or decide to recognize Me as your Lord and Savior and publicly praise and honor Me, and I will know You before My Father. Continue to praise Me in public. *Peace and blessings.*

The Gift of
Correction

Day
Two Hundred and Sixteen

You Have Not

You have not because you ask not. A short but powerful statement. The author was awakened by the Lord a few weeks ago and given this statement. I was suffering with pain from my sciatic nerve on my right side. He showed me that I had prayed for others but not for myself. I cleansed myself by asking for forgiveness and in my prayer I asked for healing and not pain relief. Praise the Lord because He gave me what I asked for. What about you? Have you asked the Lord for something realistic such as healing, pain relief, spiritual endurance, financial assistance, or maybe a job? Be sincere and realistic in what you are asking for and give God time to reply. Your timeliness is not God's time. Trust me, your answer may not be instant, but He is working on your request and He will be on time.
Peace and blessings.

Peace And Blessings : with the Risen *SON*

Day
Two Hundred and Seventeen

Upright and Blameless

To live like the Job is challenging. Let's define our title words. From a vertical position, I look down and know all your sins. Your objective is to stop sinning when you learn of your sinful actions. Blameless is horizontal. Humanity watches you and finds you blameless or no fault in you. Remember, although seen upright and blameless, there is always room for improvement. If you want to do better, connect with the Comforter (The Holy Spirit), and He will direct your path. Learn to have a respective fear of our Creator who has the power to send you to heaven or hell. You know right from wrong; avoid evil things, places, activities, and people. Continue your walk with the Holy Spirit and Me as you continue life's journey. "There is no one on earth like him; he is blameless and upright, a man who fears God and shuns evil." (NIV) Job 1:8b *Peace and blessings.*

Peace And Blessings : with the Risen *SON*

Day
Two Hundred and Eighteen

Your Adjudicator

A judge is an adjudicator who makes a ruling in a case.
When I bring everything to judgment, those matters
come before Me for a verdict. The ruling is deciding
whether you go to heaven or hell based on your life.
Once a judge chooses to, you can appeal to a higher
court. When I decide, there is no higher court of appeal.
I am your adjudicator, and My decision is final. Now is
the time to change your lifestyle before you meet Me
as your adjudicator. You must call on the Holy Spirit to
lead and guide you. I will bring every act to judgment,
everything which is hidden, whether good or bad.
Ecclesiastes 12:14 *Peace and blessings.*

Day
Two Hundred and Nineteen

Who Needs to Repent

As you read the verse at the end of this devotional, your first thought may be to list those you consider sinners. Your list may grow as you list individuals you believe are wrong and sinful. Relook at your list. Where is your name? Are you one of them? You have yet to arrive; some things may hinder your entry into my kingdom. You know, the little white lie you told so you would not hurt someone's feelings. Conduct checks and balances on your actions. Remember the school supplies you took from work for your child to use. The grapes you ate at Harris Teeter, Food Lion, or Kroger before you paid for them. I saw you returned the half-eaten bag and paid for a new one. Yes, put your name on the list of individuals who must repent. Ask the Holy Spirit to assist you in identifying your shortcomings and correcting them. I have gone to prepare a place for individuals worthy of being in my kingdom. "I have not come to call the righteous, but sinners to repentance." Luke 5:32 (NET)
Peace and blessings.

Peace And Blessings : with the Risen *SON*

Day
Two Hundred and Twenty

Imagination Versus Truth

Imagination in Scrabble gets fourteen points, but in life, you can believe in and on things that are not true. To be deceived by others is one thing, but not as bad as deceiving yourself. Imagination can make one believe they are more than they are. If there was anyone who thought himself to be something when he was nothing, it was Satan both before and after his fall. Satan – who works on and on against God in the self-delusion that he may one day triumph over God. Study the Bible so your image does not run wild, causing you to believe you are more than you are. When you accept the truth of who you are, God can elevate you to become more than you were. Never self-elevate yourself in this world that is full of deceit. Stay in step with me. You walk in the truth when you walk the path God places you. "For if a man thinks himself to be something when he is nothing, he deceived himself." Galatians 6:3 (KJV)
Peace and blessings.

Day
Two Hundred and Twenty One

Triage

Triage in the medical profession assigns the degree of urgency to wounds or illnesses to decide the treatment order for many patients or casualties. What would happen, and how would this affect you if I assigned the degree of urgency to your needs versus someone else?

In the medical field, those with difficult situations get served first. You serve and worship an all-powerful and all-present God. My Father knows your conditions, your problems, your needs, your prayers, your weaknesses, and your strengths. He does not conduct triage to determine who He needs to heal or assist. He can respond to everyone simultaneously and be on time for your situation. I need you to stop conducting triage when you need Us. The reality is you need Us (Father, Son, and The Holy Spirit) all the time, regardless of what you are doing. "News about him spread all over Syria, and people brought to him all who were ill with various diseases, those severe suffering pain, the demon-possessed, those having seizures, and the paralyzed; and he healed them. "When you call on Us, we respond, reciprocate, and answer when we call on you. Matthew 4:24 (NIV)
Peace and blessings.

Peace And Blessings : with the Risen *SON*

Day
Two Hundred and Twenty Two

5th Word from the Cross

I had not slept since I woke up Thursday morning. I had been tried and found guilty by a court of being me, beaten twice as a punishment, and beaten and spit upon by the guards. I carried that heavy cross as far as possible while the guards whipped me. A man was pulled from the crowd to help Me carry this heavy cross. I stood on the cross, and they nailed my feet to it. They laid me down, stretched my arms, and nailed my hands to the cross. The pain was unbearable. I had been on the cross for at least six hours. My shoulders ached, and my mouth was parched. I was bleeding and sweating. I said I was thirsty. Someone brought me a sponge on a stalk of a hyssop plant. Yes, I sipped a little wine vinegar, but I thirsted more to be with my Father in heaven. To return to my kingdom and enjoy the fruits of glory. Thirst does not always mean a fluid, but one can thirst for many other things. I hope you have a thirst to be with me in my kingdom. Like me, you may suffer many things to get there, but it is well worth it. I will prepare a place and return to get you. Get ready. John 19:28 "I thirst!" (KJV)

Peace and blessings.

Peace And Blessings : with the Risen *SON*

Day
Two Hundred and Twenty Three

Taking Off Sin

Satan was at the Angel's right hand, making accusations against Joshua. I wonder if Satan is making accusations against you before you arrive. He could be making accusations against you here on earth to friends, family, and co-workers. Jesus was crucified, died, and rose to give you victory over Satan. We have an advocate named Jesus. He says to take off your dirty clothes, which are your sins, and your new clothes are a new lease on life through Jesus. Daily, we should be removing sin from our lives. Daily, it would be best if you were moving closer to Me. Once cleaned, you must follow your Advocate. "Joshua's clothing was filthy as he stood there before the angel. So the angel said to the others standing there, "Take off his filthy clothes." And turning to Joshua, he said, "See, I have taken away your sins, and now I am giving you these fine new clothes." Zechariah 3:3-4 (NLT) *Peace and blessings.*

Peace And Blessings : with the Risen *SON*

Day
Two Hundred and Twenty Four

Walk with Me

Walking with Me is challenging, especially if you have yet to accept Jesus as your Savior. You can be led by every wind, doctrine, or anybody's counsel. But David says blessed is the person who avoids these people and maintains a relationship with Me. You increase your relationship with Me as you walk and talk with Me. The challenge of staying connected becomes more manageable because of your connectivity. Walking with Me is like a child walking and holding hands with their father. They feel the assurance of safety and love. Are you walking with Me, or are you like the child trying to be grown and running ahead of the family getting in trouble? Hindsight in 2020 is the time for corrective spiritual action. Change what you are doing and "Walk with Me." May the grace of God be with you. "Blessed is the man who walks not in the counsel of the wicked, nor stands in the way of sinners, nor sits in the seat of scoffers." Psalms 1:1(ESV)
Peace and blessings.

Peace And Blessings : with the Risen *SON*

Day
Two Hundred and Twenty Five

Honesty

Honesty is the quality or fact of being upright, fair, truthful, sincere, or frank; freedom from deceit or fraud." (Dictionary.com) God wants everyone to be honest and fair to each other. Do you have a reason to be unfair? God, who is unchangeable, treats all of you the same. He allows it to rain on the just as well as the unjust. A false balance deals with weights and measures. In the business world, the tare, the weight of the meat tray, the produce tray, or any item that holds something weighted, must be taken off. When it is not taken off, your product costs more.

The higher the cost, the more profit is made if the tare is not removed. God hates deceitful practices. Be fair to all in every aspect of your life, and God will bless you. "The integrity of the upright guides them, but the unfaithful are destroyed by their duplicity (deceitfulness). A false balance is an abomination to the LORD, but a just weight is his delight. Proverbs 11:3 (NIV) *Peace and blessings.*

Peace And Blessings : with the Risen *SON*

Day
Two Hundred and Twenty Six

Check Your Communication

Communication is the exchanging of information. It is not you tell me something, and I will tell you something. In a relationship, it lets a person know what is happening. I communicated with My disciples, informing them of My journey to Jerusalem to the cross. Each time I shared this information, the disciples encouraged Me not to go.

As you communicate, be conscious or aware of the tone you use. A soft tone with hard words is more acceptable than a stern tone with hard words. In your communication, choose your words and tone more carefully to bring peace and harmony, not discord. May the grace of God be with you. James 3 says, "No man can tame the tongue. It is an unruly evil, full of deadly poison." "Let the words of my mouth and the meditation of my heart be acceptable in your sight, O LORD, my rock and my redeemer." Psalm 19:14 (ESV) *Peace and blessings.*

Day
Two Hundred and Twenty Seven

Peace

As I look down, I see so many things going on. The world is far from what we designed it to be. Each generation moves farther and farther away spiritually. Life can be so simple if one would surrender themselves to me. Being submissive is challenging because most individuals cannot be under another person's authority. But I am not another person; I am your Creator; I designed you in My likeness and image. You fight with one another; you desire what others have, and your love for money makes you do sinful things. Accept the peace I am offering you so you can enjoy your once-in-a-lifetime journey on Earth. The peace I offer you is beyond human understanding. Relax, allow the Holy Spirit to guide you, and you will begin to embark or enter on your heavenly bound path that not many will accept. I am looking forward to seeing you. Peace I leave with you, my peace I give unto you: not as the world giveth, give I unto you. Let not your heart be troubled, neither let it be afraid. John 14:27 (ESV)
Peace and blessings.

Peace And Blessings : with the Risen *SON*

Day
Two Hundred and Twenty Eight

Lead or Follow

As a disciple, you must decide if you will be or become a leader or a follower. Everybody is not designed for leadership because of problems when dealing with people. Paul was a leader who faced and handled people's issues in his writings to the churches. Determine if you are better at following. There is no harm in being a follower. Followers are essential in ensuring the tasks and the missions are completed. But, if you can't or will not be either, sit and be quiet until you have something productive to bring to the table. There is a Marine bumper sticker that reads, "Lead, follow, or get the hell out of the way!" It is a bold but true statement for use in all facets of life.
Peace and blessings.

Day
Two Hundred and Twenty Nine

The Cost of Looking Back

God blessed Lot, his wife, and his daughters with the ability to escape from Sodom and Gomorrah. His sons- in-law remained to enjoy the pleasures the cities offered. When I present an opportunity to escape danger or sin, you must take it. The Angels sent Lot and his family out of the town with instructions not to look back. Once they arrived at a city called Zoar, Lot's wife looked back while the two cities were being destroyed and became a pillar of salt. Did she leave pleasures that caused her to look back? Looking back into our past can draw us back or cause our death; if not physically, it happens spiritually. Now that you have glimpsed into your past, move forward, shake the dust from your feet, and enjoy living for Me.

"But his wife looked back from behind him, and she became a pillar of salt." Genesis 19:26
Peace and blessings.

Peace And Blessings : with the Risen *SON*

Day
Two Hundred and Thirty

Walk in the Light

If you walk with Me, the world's light, you should be able to fellowship with one another. The blood I shed on the cross cleanses and covers a multitude of sins. "On this side of eternity, sinless perfection is impossible, yet you can still walk in the light. If we do not have fellowship with one another, then one or both parties are not walking in the light." (David Guzik) If you are calling yourself Christians, my disciples, why are you not a living example of a person walking in the light? When you walk in the light, you should practice "Agape, unconditional love" for one another. Walk in the beautiful light; come where the dewdrops of mercy shine bright. They shine all around us by day and night; Jesus is the world's light. Hold my hand and walk with Me.

"But if we walk in the light, as he is in the light, we have fellowship with one another, and the blood of Jesus his Son cleanses us from all sin." 1 John 1:7 (ESV) *Peace and blessings.*

Peace And Blessings : with the Risen *SON*

Day
Two Hundred and Thirty One

Casting Lots or Gambling

After they had nailed Me to the cross, the soldiers gambled for My clothes by throwing dice. Typical forms of gambling include Lottery games like lotto or lotto max, Instant games like scratch cards, bingo games, Nevada tickets, sports betting, casino games like slot machines and table games, card games, and horseracing. Individuals bet on all types of things, events, and people. Your life before and after death is not a betting matter. Do not bet on if there is heaven or hell because both are real.

Your goal is to live eternity in heaven, not hell. A sure bet is I will return to a church without a spot or blemish. Instead of betting, use your time wisely, getting ready for my return. "They said therefore among themselves, Let us not rend it, but cast lots for it, whose it shall be: that the scripture might be fulfilled, which saith, They parted my raiment among them, and for my vesture, they did cast lots. These things, therefore, the soldiers did.' John 19:24 (KJV) *Peace and blessings.*

Peace And Blessings : with the Risen *SON*

Day
Two Hundred and Thirty Two

Ignorance

Have you considered or taken the time to determine what gifts I have placed inside you? Paul makes a bold statement to the church at Corinth regarding these gifts that will enhance your life. Paul wants to give guidance on the gifts of the Spirit so you can use them in your interactions with others and even yourself. He highlights the word ignorant and how costly "not knowing" can be. Ignorance is simply being without knowledge of something. " Sometimes, we say," We do not know what we do not know." Ignorance is not a word of disrespect but a word indicating having a lack of knowledge of specific information. But we have a God who knows everything. Now concerning spiritual gifts, brethren, I would not have you ignorant. 1 Cor 12:1 (KJV) I challenge you to ask Me to show you the spaces in your life that you are ignorant in. My word tells you that people perish for not knowing things. Ask so you can live a fruitful life. ***Peace and blessings.***

Day
Two Hundred and Thirty Three

Possessions

Sell all you have and give to the poor or heaven? You would think this would be a no-brainer, but this man's challenge was that he knew of Earth and his possessions but not Heaven. His faith was in what he knew. Do not let your possessions (house, cars, property, etc.) hinder your heavenly journey. There is more in front of you than what you will leave behind. I will return soon; do not let THINGS cause you to be left behind. "Then Jesus beholding him loved him, and said unto him, one thing thou lack: go thy way, sell whatsoever thou hast, and give to the poor, and thou shalt have treasure in heaven: and come, take up the cross, and follow me. And he was sad at that saying and went away grieving, for he had great possessions. "Mark 10:21-22 (KJV) Jesus said, "I go to prepare a place for you, and if I go, I will return. John 14:3 (KJV) *Peace and blessings.*

Day
Two Hundred and Thirty Four

Stress

Don't let stress control you. Today, individuals are stressed about many situations like marriage, children, jobs, church, money, vehicles, family, and friends. How many of these things can you change? You must learn to destress because stress kills you. Destress by contemplating (thinking and talking) with Me. Please stay in your lane when someone brings you situations that don't belong to you, play tennis, and knock the ball or situation back in their court. STAY IN YOUR LANE and out of other people's business. For instance, if you can't change it, like the weather, don't stress over it. I provide comfort by giving you "My peace. ". "Peace, I leave with you; my Peace I give to you. Not as the world gives do I give to you. Let not your hearts be troubled, neither let them be afraid. "John 14:27 (NIV) *Peace and blessings.*

Day
Two Hundred and Thirty Five

Sphere of Influence

I define power as having command, control, and a sphere of influence over individuals. Today, the power to control people makes political individuals feel they are at the top of their game. I had the power of influence. I told My disciples to follow Me, and they stopped what they were doing and followed. I used My power of influence to win souls. Do you have the power of influence? Do you use it correctly? An ingredient of power is respect. Your sphere of influence is a powerful tool in leadership. Do you curse people to get them to respond to you? Do others under you respect you? Do you respect them? Your words, actions, deeds, and respect for others are part of your sphere of influence; do not abuse it. ""Levi the publican was working, and Jesus said, "Follow me," and he rose and followed. Luke 5:24-28 (CSB) *Peace and blessings.*

Peace And Blessings : with the Risen *SON*

Day
Two Hundred and Thirty Six

Speak Up

There are instances where you see wrong in action and are helpless to stop this adverse action. How often did you not step up to correct something wrong? As Christians, you cannot allow your legs or spirit to become stiff or non-movable when you see wrongdoing or sin. Let the Holy Spirit guide you on what to say, how to say it, and when to move. Paul was speechless because he persecuted Christians, and this situation may have been a motivator. Allow the Holy Spirit to be your motivator and push you into action. Besides the Holy Spirit, a disciple's most incredible tool is the voice: stand up and speak up. "And when the blood of your witness Stephen was shed, I was standing nearby? Acts 22:10 (NASB) *Peace and blessings.*

Day
Two Hundred and Thirty Seven

Sins of Omission and Commission

Many passages of scripture warn against doing certain things. "These warnings, and many others like them, describe sins of commission. Sins of commission are overt (committed openly) sinful acts. David taking Bathsheba is an example of a sin of commission (II Samuel 11). It was sinful because it was something David was not supposed to do. On the other hand, a sin of omission is an act left undone, something I expect you to do but don't. In the parable of the Good Samaritan, the Priest and the Levite sinned through omission by not assisting the hurt man (Luke 10:25-37, KJV).

When you take a serious look at yourself, there are both types of sins in your life. The goal is to decrease both with particular emphasis on the sins of commission, which are seen openly. These sins influence others: "church folks are doing the same thing you are doing." Be advised that sin is sin in My eyes. It separates you from Me. Move forward as sinlessly as possible today. You shall have no other gods before Me." "You shall not take the name of the Lord your God in vain." "You shall not murder. You shall not commit adultery. You shall not steal" Ex. 20:3, 7, 13- 15 (KJV).
Peace and blessings.

Peace And Blessings : with the Risen *SON*

Day
Two Hundred and Thirty Eight

Learn of Me

Paul writes a letter to the Philippians to enhance their growth and knowledge in Jesus. They were converted from various beliefs, and some had no religious beliefs. He is praying that their former beliefs and thoughts are removed to propel them forward, seeking Jesus as Savior and Lord. It was very challenging since, in their understanding, Rome had Caesar as King, and Jesus was now their new spiritual King. The more the Philippians learn in this new religion, the greater their faith and the more they will be pure and blameless when Christ returns. You are like the Philippians, needing to learn more about Me, Jesus, your Savior. Today, your King appears to be the electronic gadget you enjoy and do not want to live without. But I am more significant than your gadgets, social media, and humanity. When you learn of Me, you gain inner peace, a spiritual understanding beyond humanity's comprehension. Pray for spiritual growth.

"And this is my prayer: that your love may abound more and more in knowledge and depth of insight so that you may be able to discern what is best and may be pure and blameless for the day of Christ," Philippians 1:9-10 (NIV)
Peace and blessings.

Peace And Blessings : with the Risen *SON*

Day
Two Hundred and Thirty Nine

Nothing to Boast About

Boasting is talking with excessive pride and self-satisfaction about one's achievements, possessions, or abilities. What have we to boast about when it comes to our justification, our righteousness, or our salvation? Humanity could achieve nothing without God's grace through His Son Jesus. Therefore, boasting should and must be eliminated. Boasting should be on how God chose to give you salvation. I have given you three translations of Roman 3:27 to bring a more precise understanding. "Where is boasting then? It is excluded. By what law? of works? Nay: but by the law of faith. "Roman 3:27 (KJV) "So, do we have anything to brag about? Bragging has been eliminated. On what basis was it eliminated? Based on our efforts? No, indeed! Rather, it is eliminated based on faith." (GWT) "Can we boast, then, that we have done anything to be accepted by God? No, because our acquittal is not based on obeying the law. It is based on faith."(NLT). Wow, that's a lot to engulf, but so is salvation.
Peace and blessings.

Peace And Blessings : with the Risen *SON*

Day
Two Hundred and Forty

True North vs Magnetic North

A compass is used to assist you in traveling in a direction. Magnetic North is used on the compass because of the Earth's magnetic pull. There are two North Poles, the Magnetic North Pole, and the True North Pole. The difference in distance is three hundred-eleven miles.

The farther you travel using magnetic north, the greater the distance to true north. Look at magnetic north as humanity's nature to sin and true north as being on the road called straight. The magnetic pull to sin is strong; many travelers take this journey. The further you travel, the greater the distance to cross to true north. When you find Me, Jesus, you will find True North with peace and blessings as we travel together to My kingdom. "Enter through the narrow gate. For wide is the gate, broad is the road that leads to destruction, and many enter through it. But small is the gate and narrow the road that leads to life, and only a few find it." Matthew 7:13-14 (NIV) *Peace and blessings.*

Peace And Blessings : with the Risen *SON*

Day
Two Hundred and Forty One

Spiritual Perfection

Perfection is being free or accessible from all flaws or defects. Perfection is an individual with no impurities on the skin, no cracked or crooked teeth, no scars, and a perfectly shaped head. No one is perfect physically or spiritually. No one is sinless. To reach perfection, you need Me, Jesus, so you can enjoy what I have prepared for you. Everything will be perfect, and so will you. Let both of us work on your spiritual imperfections, enhancing your eternal life opportunity. Life in my kingdom is out of this world. "As it is written: "There is no one righteous, not even one." Who do you know that is physically perfect? Romans 3:10 (NIV) Eye have not seen or ear heard, neither have entered into the heart of man, the things which I have prepared for them that love Me. Corinthians 2:9 (KJV) *Peace and blessings.*

Day
Two Hundred and Forty Two

Humble Pie

Humble pie is a figurative serving of humiliation, usually in forced submission, apology, or retraction. Have you ever met someone who never apologizes for their mistakes but always wants you to own them? Are you a victim of having to eat humble pie? To avoid eating humble pie, be upfront in your dealings with people. Be the first to apologize. Listen to and follow the guidance of the Holy Spirit. Become wise by watching others eat humble pie so you do not have to. Humble pie is unfavorable, and you feel the pain emotionally. Walk with me; I have prepared no humble pie at the table for you. With humility comes wisdom. To avoid eating humble pie, follow the second greatest commandment, "Love others as I have loved you". "When pride comes, then comes disgrace, but with humility comes wisdom." Proverbs 11:2 (NET)
Peace and blessings.

Peace And Blessings : with the Risen *SON*

Day
Two Hundred and Forty Three

Judging Others

You think you can condemn people you consider sinful,
but you are just as sinful, and you have no excuse
because you should know better. When you say they are
wicked and should be punished, you condemn yourself,
for you who judge others do these very same things. It
is amazing how you judge others without realizing how
much you are like them. When allowed to lead, you lead
using the same criteria as those before you, but you are
far worse because you want to be better, but you use the
old model. Look for the positive in people just as I,
Jesus, do you. I see and know your sins, but I still love
you, not your sinful nature. Therefore, accept Me as
your Savior, and I will teach you how to stay connected
to me and not become judge and jury of others. "You
hypocrite, first take the plank out of your eye, and then
you will see clearly to remove the speck from your
brother's eye." Matthew 7:5 (NIV)
Peace and blessings.

Peace And Blessings : with the Risen *SON*

Day
Two Hundred and Forty Four

Sinful Nature

Romans 8:6 (NLT) says, "So letting your sinful nature control your mind leads to death. But letting the Spirit control your mind leads to life and peace." When reading the New Testament, you are reading about newly established churches. The irony is that our present-day churches are dealing with the same issues. Do not allow your old sinful nature to rule or control you because that leads to spiritual death. "A physical death is the separation of the soul from the body. Spiritual death, which is of greater significance, is the separation of the soul from God." Accept Me, as your Lord and Savior, read and study the Bible, meditate, and pray daily. When you accomplish these tasks, you push your sinful nature away and allow the Holy Spirit to bring joy and peace as you pursue eternal life. When you walk beside and with me, I can help you along your journey. *Peace and blessings.*

Day
Two Hundred and Forty Five

Evicting the Enemy

An eviction is a civil process by which a landlord may legally remove a tenant from their rental property.

Do you recall Me, Jesus, evicting the devil from individuals? Matthew 4:16 (KJV) When evening came, they brought to Him many demon-possessed; and He cast out the spirits with a word, and healed all who were ill. Luke 11:14 (KJV) And He was casting out a demon, and it was mute; when the demon had gone out, the mute man spoke, and the crowds were amazed. There are more cases where I evicted devils from humans. Do not allow the demon to return. Then it takes seven other spirits more wicked than itself, and they go in and live there. And the final condition of that person is worse than the first. Read, study, and contemplate to fight the return of the enemy. Hold My hand and walk with Me so the demons do not return. I will not leave or forsake you in your time of need. ***Peace and blessings.***

Peace And Blessings : with the Risen *SON*

Day
Two Hundred and Forty Six

Love

Love occurs in 281 verses in the King James Version and 447 times in the New English Translation. Love is an intense feeling of deep affection. There are various types of love, but you allow this word to slip out of your lips so freely and meaninglessly. Who knows which meaning you are expressing when you say I love you? From my point of view, if you love me, you need to show some signs. Your love cannot be asymptomatic (without signs).

Loving you is easy, even when you are wrong. I continue not just to say I love you, but I also express it in my actions. My Father loves you so much that he allowed me to bear your sins on the cross where I was crucified. God so loved the world that he gave his only Son (Me), that whoever believes in Me should not perish but have eternal life. So, when I say I love you, it is words and love in action. My love for you is not asymptomatic (without signs). ***Peace and blessings.***

Day
Two Hundred and Forty Seven

If

"If" is a big little word (KJV). John 14:15 "If ye love me, keep my commandments. NLT) If you love me, obey my commandments." Both translations say love me. King James says keep, and the New Living Translation says obey. When you love someone, you do all you can to please them. "If" is a condition or supposition. Suppose it carries with it a caveat, a condition. In this scripture, love is the most important word. I want you to do what you are supposed to do out of love and not feel forced to do it.

You will keep and obey my commandment because you love me. As a Christian, everything you do for me and others should be done out of love. Doing things out of love makes your tasks much more accessible to complete. I told Peter, if you love me, feed my sheep. If you love Me, strip yourself as much as you can of sin or any hindrance to loving Me. The more you love me, the less you will sin. Put your love for me into action by obeying my commandments and loving others as I have loved you. If, a big little word. ***Peace and blessings.***

Peace And Blessings : with the Risen *SON*

Day
Two Hundred and Forty Eight

Do You Love Your Neighbor?

"But he, willing to justify himself, said unto Jesus, And
who is my neighbor?" Luke 10:29

A common identification of a neighbor is the person
living next door to you. Do you love the person next
door to you, or do you love other community members?
When asked who my neighbor in this scripture, I gave a
parable to help this young man obtain an answer.
Three individuals passed a man robbed and beaten, but
only one stopped to help this man. Was his neighbor the
one who helped him because he showed compassion?
When engaged in the second greatest commandment,
"Do unto others as you would have them do unto you,"
your neighbor can be anyone on this Earth. Neighbors
must not be selected by the color of their eyes, skin,
nationality, beliefs, or religion. If you use that process,
you are prejudiced and have selective neighbors. You
can love your neighbor and hate or dislike their actions
or activities. Love your neighbor with their faults as I
have loved you with all your faults.
Peace and blessings.

Peace And Blessings : with the Risen *SON*

Day
Two Hundred and Forty Nine

I Love You on Purpose

Romans 8:38-39 says, "For I am persuaded that neither death nor life, nor angels nor principalities nor powers, nor things present nor things to come, nor height nor depth, nor any other created thing, shall be able to separate us from the love of God which is in Christ Jesus our Lord."

I created you to worship me in spirit and truth freely. I did not force you to worship or love me. Regardless of your feelings toward me, I purposely love you. Even when you sin, I hate sin but still love the individual. I could stop you from sinning, but I gave you free will to choose what you want to do. As a Christian, one of my disciples and followers, nothing can separate you from my love. I adore you; my love for you is more significant than you can envision. Increase your time with me, get to know me better every day, and you will begin to see that I love you on purpose. Try to love those on Earth as I have loved you. Be forgiving, kindhearted, and as loving as I have been to others, and you will begin to understand my love for you. More significant is that he is in you than he that is in the world. *Peace and blessings.*

Peace And Blessings : with the Risen *SON*

Day
Two Hundred and Fifty

Reciprocate

"A new command I give you: Love one another. As I have loved you, so you must love one another." John 13:34 (NIV)

I taught my disciples the importance of love through this new commandment. To love others just like I loved them. Reciprocate means to respond to a gesture or action by making a corresponding one: to do (something) for or to someone who has done something similar for or to you. I loved my disciples; therefore, I wanted them to love others. I turned things around with the second greatest commandment; "Do unto others as you want them to do unto you." First, they were to love others because I loved them; now, they are to as you want other to do. Regardless of how the disciples went in either commandment, they reciprocated what I taught them and taught others the importance of reciprocation. The more you treat others like you want to be treated, the better your relationship with each other and Me will be. Reciprocate my love for you and watch your actions toward others. *Peace and blessings.*

Peace And Blessings : with the Risen *SON*

Day
Two Hundred and Fifty One

3rd Words From the Cross

"Woman, behold thy son! Behold thy mother." John 19:26 (KJV)

Do you find it strange that I would give my mother away while on the cross? Do you understand the custom during that time? A woman without a husband or a son to care for her could not survive. John was the only disciple at the cross. I left my mother in the care of a believer who could and would love her as his mother. I called her woman out of respect. Calling her mother would enhance her troubles. My departure time was approaching, and I needed her in the best care. The scriptures say we are to honor our Father and Mother. Joseph, Mary's husband, is dead. Parents are expected to die before their children. I honor my earthly mother by ensuring she has someone to care for her when I am gone. I have nothing to leave her except my love. Even the guards threw dice for my coat. Nevertheless, I've left my mother in great hands, and she will be exceptionally cared for. Follow my example and take care of your parents. ***Peace and blessings.***

Peace And Blessings : with the Risen *SON*

Day Two Hundred and Fifty Two

Loving You is Easy

Judas dipped in with me, identified as the traitor, and was told to be about his business. Judas proved himself a false brother, but the other disciples and you must not harbor such jealousies and suspicions of one another. Doing so would put distress in loving one another even though there was one traitor among them, yet not all are Judases.

Knowing the potential to hate was in the air, I shared a new commandment with the eleven. A commandment is a divine rule. It isn't that this commandment was just invented, but it was presented in a new, fresh way. New implies freshness or the opposite of 'outworn' rather than simply 'recent' or 'different.' Can you love one another as I have loved you? Loving others is difficult, but remember, I loved you despite your many faults and sins. I loved you unconditionally. Do the same to others.
Peace and blessings.

Peace And Blessings : with the Risen *SON*

Day Two Hundred and Fifty Three

Greatest Commandment

My Father wrote the Ten Commandments for Moses to give to the Israelites. The first four pertain to your relationship with My Father. I modified those commandments into one, and this is how it reads. Love the Lord your God with all your heart, with all your soul, and with all your mind. It is the greatest and most important commandment. If you do this, then you will not put anything before God. You must honor and put God First in everything you do, and God will be pleased.

We created you to worship and praise God, so you were created to do and enjoy a wonderful life on earth and in heaven. *Peace and blessings.*

Peace And Blessings : with the Risen *SON*

Day
Two Hundred and Fifty Four

Second Greatest Commandment

The second is like the greatest commandment. It is the short version of the last six commandments about your relationship with one another. Love your neighbor as yourself. Another version of this commandment is to "Do unto others as you would have them do unto you." You know you must love yourself first to love others. Individuals who do not love themselves display hate and anger toward others. I love you with all your faults or sins. Others love you with your faults, but you can't love them. Treat others the way you want to be treated. Why are you mean to others and want them to give you royal treatment? An old saying is, "What is good for the goose is good for the gander." It means treating all people the same. My treatment of you is always the same; reciprocate my treatment of you and to you to others in your life. Do unto others as you would have them do unto you. It is the right thing to do.
Peace and blessings.

Peace And Blessings : with the Risen *SON*

Day
Two Hundred and Fifty Five

Love in Action

"Love must be sincere. Hate what is evil; cling to what is good." Romans 12:9 (NIV)

As Christians, you must put love into action. Much of what masquerades as "love" in the Christian community is laced with hypocrisy (claiming to have higher standards than others) and must be demonstrated against.

Love is patient; love is kind. It does not envy; it does not boast; it is not proud. It does not dishonor others, is not self-seeking, is not easily angered, and keeps no record of wrongs. Love does not delight in evil but rejoices with the truth. It always protects, always trusts, always hopes, and always perseveres. True love never fails. Your love must be put into action because actions speak louder than words. I love you unconditionally despite your sins. I hate sin. Can you do the same for others? *Peace and blesssings.*

Peace And Blessings : with the Risen *SON*

Day
Two Hundred and Fifty Six

Real Love

Romans 13:9 (KJV)" Thou shalt love thy neighbor
as thyself." Paul speaks of various commandments
in verse 9 and sums up these with the above verse.
Society teaches us to take care of ourselves first before
others. If one loves oneself, this is the perfect example
of loving others the same way we love ourselves. We
will do nothing to harm ourselves purposely. Who is
your neighbor? Your neighbor becomes anyone but
you, which makes everyone your neighbor. Love is the
fulfillment of the law, which makes or causes you to go
beyond the law's requirement and follow Me. 1 Peter
4:8 (NLT) Most crucial of all, continue to show deep
love for each other, for love covers a multitude of sins."
When we have real love, love covers a lot of the sins of
others, which decreases the harsh effect or magnitude of
what may have occurred. Is loving others challenging?
Yes. Although difficult, can we love others? Yes. To
love you as I love myself, you are loved.
Peace and blessings.

Peace And Blessings : with the Risen *SON*

Day
Two Hundred and Fifty Seven

Loving Others

1 Thessalonians 3:12 (NET) says, "And may the Lord cause you to increase and abound in love for one another and for all, just as we do for you," Paul writes to the Thessalonians about growing, thriving, prospering, and maturing in love for one another. As you grow in love, you are strengthened in holiness and will grow closer to me. Your love of Me is the key to your maturity, spiritual growth, and relationship. The closer we become, the more blameless you are. Love must begin in My family. You learn to love not just individuals who love you but everyone. Others will know that you are My disciples if you love one another. Remember, love others unconditionally as I have loved you. Love also enhances, increases, promotes forgiveness, and restores relationships.
Peace and blessings.

Day
Two Hundred and Fifty Eight

Covered by Love

1 Peter 4:8 (NIV) says, "Above all, love each other deeply, because love covers a multitude of sins." Have you ever watched a couple in love and saw how much they did not see about each other? Love blinded their weight gain, crooked teeth, gray hair, improper speech, and so much more. Because I love you unconditionally, the only flaw I see in you is sin, and when you ask for forgiveness, that flaw is gone. Love covers a multitude of sins. What does your love for others overlook? What does their love for you overlook? If you could read their minds, you would be amazed at how much is forgotten about you. The pot cannot call the kettle black because both are black. Love others as I have loved you. Love covers a multitude of your flaws. *Peace and blessings.*

Day
Two Hundred and Fifty Nine

Agape Love

"A new command I give you: Love one another. As I have loved you, so you must love one another." John 13:34 (NIV)

Agape is a selfless, unconditional, often universal love. Let's define agape love through scripture. For God loved the world so much that he gave his one and only Son so that everyone who believes in him will not perish but have eternal life. There is no greater love than to lay down one's life for one's friends. God demonstrated his agape for us in this: while we were still sinners, the Messiah died for us." Love is patient and kind. Love is not jealous or boastful or proud or rude. It does not demand its way. It is not irritable, and it keeps no record of being wronged. It does not rejoice about injustice but rejoices whenever the truth wins out. Love never gives up, never loses faith, is always hopeful, and endures through every circumstance. Can you reciprocate my unconditional love to others as I have loved you? Work to reciprocate agape love to others.
Peace and blessings.

Peace And Blessings : with the Risen *SON*

Day
Two Hundred and Sixty

It is Not Color Coded

"For God so loved the world, that he gave his only begotten Son, that whosoever believeth in him should not perish, but have everlasting life." John 3:16 (KJV)

I made this powerful statement many years ago, and it is still relevant to humanity today. I did not say this to a particular race of people but to everyone. Some individuals believe that no one can be a Christian but their race. Scripture does not support that statement. I love everyone I created, but not their sinful nature. God sent His only begotten Son (Me, Jesus) to die as a ransom for your sins. The caveat to the above scripture is that it is incumbent on the individual to believe in Me, Jesus, that they should not perish but have everlasting life. No, the message is not color-coded but individualized. It is addressed to everyone. No matter how you scrutinize this scripture, the ball is in your court; in plain English, you decide your eternity or fate. As you continue your life's journey, please get to know me personally while you have time.
Peace and blessings.

Day Two Hundred and Sixty One

Pray for your Enemies

"You have heard the law that says, Love your neighbor and hate your enemies. But I say, love your enemies! Pray for those who persecute you!" Matthew 5:43-44 (NLT)

It sounds so wild to pray for your enemies and those against you. There will always be individuals who are against you. Throughout My ministry, I had enemies. Indeed, you should not expect less. But the word is to love and be friendly and kind to them. You show the love I taught you to love others as I have loved you. More significant is he that is in you than he that is in the world. The Comforter should be in you, guiding, teaching, and allowing you to do great things. You must be counterintuitive and do the unexpected by praying for those who dislike you, hate you, or even have desires to kill you. By you killing them with kindness, I will draw them into Me. Do as I have commanded you, and I will take care of the rest. *Peace and blessings.*

Peace And Blessings : with the Risen *SON*

Day
Two Hundred and Sixty Two

Your First Love

Revelation 2:4 (KJV) say, "Nevertheless I have somewhat against thee because thou hast left thy first love." You left— not lost — Me, your first love. You once had a love that you don't have anymore. The distinction between leaving and losing is important. Something can be lost quite by accident, but leaving is a deliberate act, though it may not happen suddenly. When you lose something you don't know where to find it; but when you leave something, you know where to find it. Nevertheless, you have an opportunity to correct your mistake. You know where to find me because I have not left or forsaken you. I am always present, close by, within reach, just a spoken word away, or behind a door or heart waiting for you to open. I am not in the lost and found box, but next to your hard heart, knocking on the door. Open your heart, let me in so we can fellowship together. Come back to your first love, I am waiting for you. *Peace and blessings.*

Peace And Blessings : with the Risen *SON*

Day
Two Hundred and Sixty Three

What is This?

Let me share a few lines from a Walter Hawkins song. What is this? "What is this? That I feel deep inside that keeps setting my soul afire. It makes me love all my enemies, and it makes me love my friends. And it won't let me be ashamed to tell the world I've been born again. That makes me do right when I would do wrong. What is this? When I'm down low, it gives me a song. Whatever it is, it won't let me hold my peace." Can you feel the energy of this song? He is singing about the Holy Spirit and the effect the Holy Spirit has on him. What about you? Is the Holy Spirit in you, and are you allowing the Holy Spirit to take charge of you? Allow the Holy Spirit to take you to a more profound closeness with Me, Jesus, and out of your comfort zone. The Holy Spirit will make you counterintuitive, going against the norms in society, such as loving instead of hating. Let's continue your journey together. ***Peace and blessings.***

Peace And Blessings : with the Risen *SON*

Day
Two Hundred and Sixty Four

Walk in the Light

"Everyone who does evil hates the light, and will not come into the light for fear that their deeds will be exposed." John 3:20 (NIV)

Some individuals are day people while others are night people. Their preference may be job driven. But there are night people who conduct their evil deeds the cover of darkness. I need to inform everyone there is no difference for Me because I see in darkness as if it is daytime. Darkness is also for individuals who do things behind closed doors. Nevertheless, you will be exposed. I challenge you to walk and conduct business in the light, in the open, above board, so no assumptions are made. When you connect with Me, your desire must be to please Me by doing things correctly. Connect with Me, and I will light your path and destination. When challenges come, I will not leave nor forsake you. Hold My hand and let us walk together. *Peace and blessings.*

Peace And Blessings : with the Risen *SON*

Your Season is
Changing!

Embrace and Prepare for the Change

Spiritual Growth

This season focuses on your spiritual growth and your being accountable on purpose. You will deal with forgiveness from different angles, but most importantly, you will learn that forgiveness is for the forgiver. I will guide you through Satan's temptations as he tests your commitment to Me. I will not leave or forsake you; hold My hand, and we will continue your journey together.

During this season, you will explore the following subtopics:

Forgiveness: The Unseen Miracle

Temptation: A Choice and Commitment While

Overcoming Relationships

Forgiveness

Day
Two Hundred and Sixty Five

Unconditional Forgiveness

The highest type of forgiveness you can offer someone who has hurt you is unconditional forgiveness. When you forgive unconditionally, you stop basing your actions, thoughts, and feelings on what the other person said or did to hurt you. You do not attach any conditions to resuming the relationship before the hurt. You give the offender a fresh start, dispense with resentment, and go about things as if the hurt never happened. You put it in the past and let it fade away.

Unconditional forgiveness works best when the person who hurt you expresses true repentance, and you are confident the hurtful behavior will not be repeated. While unconditional forgiveness is essentially complete, it is not an open invitation for someone to hurt you again, and it does not mean you forget the hurt completely. It's more like the court system often forgives a first-time offender, sparing them a criminal conviction but keeping a private record of the original offense to ensure that a subsequent offense will be treated as a repeat.

Accept me as your Savior; you can achieve forgiveness as I forgave you. With me, there are no degrees or conditions of forgiveness, just forgiveness. "Father, forgive them, for they know not what they are doing." Luke 23:34 (KJV)
Peace and blessings.

Peace And Blessings : with the Risen *SON*

Day
Two Hundred and Sixty Six

Church Hurt

There are individuals in the church who are dealing with church hurt. Church hurt is speaking negatively about others, telling sensitive information others share with you, doing things against individuals, not asking for forgiveness, and hindering the growth of members and the membership. These are a few things, but there are more. When church hurt occurs, hurt individuals talk against the church more than the person who caused the hurt. Nevertheless, trust me, and I will help you overcome your hurt. We walk through your pain together. First, you must forgive to relieve the internal hurt and pain. When you forgive, an enormous weight is lifted off you. Do not go for revenge because revenge is mine, said the Lord.

Pray for the individual(s) causing the problem; you will be blessed. You are not the first person dealing with this; it is a trick of the enemy trying to isolate. Remember, you can do everything through me because I will strengthen you. ***Peace and blessings.***

Peace And Blessings : with the Risen *SON*

Day Two Hundred and Sixty Seven

Without Spots or Wrinkles

The idea is a body perfectly free from blemish, a soul perfectly delivered from sin, and a character perfected in all grace and goodness. It should be holy and without blemish. To be holy and without blemish, you need My forgiveness. A stain is a spot, fault, blemish, defect, or disgrace. A wrinkle is a spiritual defect or flaw. Ironically, you were created perfectly but allowed sin to invade your lives. What can you do to remove spots and wrinkles preventing you from entering heaven? Connect with Me so I can remove all stains and wrinkles. The more the Holy Spirit enters your life, the fewer spots (sins) and fewer wrinkles (folds, ridges, or creases) where sin can hide. Thank you, Holy Spirit. "That he might present it to himself a glorious church, not having spot, or wrinkle, or any such thing; but that it should be holy and without blemish. (KJV.) Ephesians 5:27 *Peace and blessings.*

Day
Two Hundred and Sixty Eight

1st Word from the Cross

The first words I spoke while crucified on the cross were important. I could have said many other things, but forgiveness mends relationships. I taught my disciples to forgive because Peter asked if forgiving seven times was enough. Seven is a start, but seventy times seven was shared for them to understand there is no number of times to forgive a person. When you forgive, the burden is lifted off you, and you can continue your life's journey. As you pray, ask my Father to forgive you; as you forgive others, He will forgive you. To relieve your stress, forgive; to grow as one of my disciples, forgive; if you want to be blessed, forgive. Forgiveness must be incorporated in all facets of your life so your relationship with my Father will blossom, grow, mature, and become enhanced. To forgive or not to forgive is a choice you must make. If you are one of my disciples, the option will be easy.

Father, forgive them, for they know not what they do.
Luke 23:34 (KJV) *Peace and blessings.*

Peace And Blessings : with the Risen *SON*

Day
Two Hundred and Sixty Nine

Grace and Mercy

You are blessed because I did not repay you for the total
cost of your sins. I had grace and mercy on you — more
mercy than grace. Mercy is not receiving the full punishment
for the crime or sin you committed. Unlike humanity,
you are given full punishment, and your record is never
cleaned. When a man calls your name, that crime or sin you
committed twenty years ago is still held against you, and you
completed the penalty. Stop holding individuals to their past.
If you can't, your past is coming back to haunt you. Have
mercy and release them from their past so that My mercy is
not removed from you.

Grace is asking for something from me and getting
more than you requested. Mercy is not receiving the full
punishment you deserve. Treat others as I treat you. "He hath
not dealt with us after our sins, nor rewarded us according to
our iniquities. (KJV) He does not punish us for all our sins;
he does not deal harshly with us, as we deserve. (NLT) "He
does not treat us as our sins deserve or repay us according to
our iniquities." (NIV) Psalms 103:10 *Peace and blessings.*

Peace And Blessings : with the Risen *SON*

Day
Two Hundred and Seventy

Forgiveness Seventy Times Seven

Peter asked a question about Me that many individuals ask. To forgive seven times was considered excellent since seven was their number of completions. But I took a different path: forgive 70 times 7. But my real message is not to limit how often you forgive a person when they ask, even if it is for the same offense. When on the cross, My first words were, "Father, forgive them, for they know not what they do." That is such a strong statement! It mends broken relationships, shows the God in you, brings sinners to Me, and gives you peace. It brings us closer together. But there is one thing I'd like you to consider, one thing to keep in mind. I did not give you an expiration or maximum number of times to forgive. Whew, I know that is heavy. But your challenge is to FORGIVE, over and over again.

Forgiveness is for the forgiver. If you don't, you will suffer because you carry extra baggage. Then came Peter to Me and said, Lord, how oft shall my brother sin against me, and I forgive him? till seven times? I told him, not until seven times: but, Until seventy times seven. Matthew 18:21-22 (KJV) *Peace and blessings.*

Peace And Blessings : with the Risen *SON*

Day Two Hundred and Seventy One

Will Thou be Made Whole?

A powerful question I asked this laned man. It may be implied or assumed that this man had control of his destiny but lacked trust and faith in Me. As you look at Me conducting miracles, this question or a similar one was asked. Individuals accepted this question, seeking healing from their infirmaries or sickness. But this question was two-fold, which also includes forgiveness of sins. I usually told those I healed only to go to the temple to make the proper sacrifice and to go and sin no more. When a healing of this magnitude occurs, you can't keep it to yourself. I asked you this same question; "Will you be made whole?" No response is required from me, but I am listening. Don't wait too long if you have not decided; I will return soon. "When Jesus saw him lie, and knew that he had been now a long time in that case, he saith unto him, Wilt thou be made whole?" John 5:6 (KJV) *Peace and blessings.*

Peace And Blessings : with the Risen *SON*

Day
Two Hundred and Seventy Two

Unrequested Forgiveness

"Then said Jesus, Father, forgive them; for they know not what they do." Luke 23:34a (KJV)

I did nothing wrong but was crucified. I asked for those who treated me wrong to be forgiven. Forgiveness is for the forgiver. By asking for their forgiveness, I released myself from the burden of them not asking. You may find yourself in the same situation. Someone has hurt you, treated you badly, and continued in life like nothing happened. You feel the pain, the hurt and the frustration, the aggravation of seeing them, and in the need to retaliate. Show Me in you by asking the Holy Spirit to help you forgive. Do not do evil for evil because then you have become them. No, that individual will not ask for forgiveness because they want to see you walking around suffering and waiting for them to ask.

Release your pain and suffering by forgiving. When you really forgive, you smile when you see them and have joy beyond their understanding. No, you did not forget what happened, it was the Holy Spirit that brought you through the pain and suffering. Rebuild your trust in them, but it will never be at the past level. Yes, they may never ask for forgiveness, but forgive, move forward, and be an example, and you will be blessed. Do something counterintuitive; you forgive. ***Peace and blessings.***

Peace And Blessings : with the Risen *SON*

Day
Two Hundred and Seventy Three

Self Forgiveness

When you ask for forgiveness, do you put yourself in a good place within yourself? You know you have been forgiven, and you roll forward in life. Satan wants you to feel guilty about past regrets, mistakes, errors, and sins.

His tactic is to make you feel that I have not forgiven you. He will tell you that you are not forgiven. He works on your pride of not wanting others to know you sinned. When a person blackmails you, they threaten to tell others of something you did that you do not want them to know. Do not allow this to happen to you because I already know everything about you. His tactic is to make you feel unforgiven. Do not allow Satan to play with your emotions, your mind, or your heart. Forgive yourself because I have forgiven you. Stop having a pity party and rejoice, shout hallelujah, and sing praises so Satan will exit your space. You asked for forgiveness, and I forgave you. Have a party rejoicing in Me, who has unconditional love for you. Others are dealing with self-forgiveness, but I have not left or forsaken you or them. Allow my love to comfort you and console you. ***Peace and blessings.***

Peace And Blessings : with the Risen *SON*

Day
Two Hundred and Seventy Four

Clemency vs Forgiveness

Clemency does not forgive you of your sin(s). I paid it all, All to Me you owe; Sin had left a crimson stain, and I washed it white as snow. Luke 23:24a "Jesus said, "Father, forgive them, for they do not know what they are doing." Before they crucified Me, the people could pardon or give Me clemency, but that was not in My Father's plan. My blood had to be shed for mankind's sins. All had sinned and fell short of the glory of God. Humanity cannot pardon or give clemency for your sins. What can wash away your sin? Nothing but the blood of Jesus; What can make you whole again? Nothing but the blood I shed. When you accept Me as your Savior, your sins are forgiven because My blood was shed for you. Stop burning precious time and accept Me now while you still have time, and I will give you forgiveness which is greater than clemency.
Peace and blessings.

Day
Two Hundred and Seventy Five

Forgiveness Summary

I shared three of man's thoughts or ideas of forgiveness with you. Unconditional forgiveness, conditional forgiveness, and dismissive forgiveness, each being a great start in the forgiveness process. Neither completely forgives, and each holds on to what occurred. Some of you are not ready to forgive because of the hurt and pain you have gone through. The more you hold on to it, the heavier the load and the more pain and hurt you endure.

Pray for total forgiveness as I gave to you. NKJV Psalms 103:12 "As far as the east is from the west, so far has He removed our transgressions from us." In this scripture, the East never meets the West; therefore, when my Father forgives your sins, he forgets them; He does not hold on to them, and never brings them up again, but man does. Release the pain seriously, forgive that person, and get a new lease on life. Vengeance is mine, said the Lord, and I do not require your assistance.
Peace and blessings.

Peace And Blessings : with the Risen *SON*

Day Two Hundred and Seventy Six

Unconditional Forgiveness

The highest type of forgiveness you can offer someone who has hurt you is unconditional forgiveness. When you forgive unconditionally, it means you stop basing your actions, thoughts, and feelings on what the person said or did to hurt you, and you do not attach any conditions to resuming the relationship as before the hurt. You give the offender a fresh start, dispense with resentment, and go about things as if the hurt never happened. You put it in the past and let it fade away. Unconditional forgiveness works best when the person who hurt you truly repents, and you are highly confident the hurtful behavior will not be repeated.

While unconditional forgiveness is essentially complete, it is not an open invitation for someone to hurt you again, and it does not mean you forget the hurt completely. You should pray that the person will not become a repeat offender. Accept me as your savior, and you can achieve forgiveness as I forgave you. With me, there are no degrees or conditions of forgiveness, just forgiveness because sin is sin. ***Peace and blessings.***

 Peace And Blessings : with the Risen *SON*

Day
Two Hundred and Seventy Seven

Repeat Offenders

"Even if that person wrongs you seven times a day and each time turns again and asks forgiveness, you must forgive." Luke 17:4 (NLT)

Forgiveness is a challenging task that I mandated to my disciples. Now, I am challenging you to forgive. Family and close friends make it difficult to forgive because you trusted them. Release yourself from this burden by forgiving them. Take them off your hook and put them on My hook so I can deal with them. When I told Peter to forgive a person seventy times seven, the caveat to that message was to forgive regardless of the number of times. Yes, they may be repeat offenders doing the same thing repeatedly, but if they ask for forgiveness, forgive them. You forgive them, and I will chasten them as required. You asked Me for forgiveness, and I forgave you unconditionally. Reciprocate Forgiveness, and you will be forgiven.
Peace and blessings.

Peace And Blessings : with the Risen *SON*

Day
Two Hundred and Seventy Eight

When Sins are Forgiven

Psalms 32:1 (NIV) Says, "Blessed is the one whose transgressions are forgiven, whose sins are covered." I told Isaiah, I, even I, am he who blots out your transgressions, for my own sake, and remembers your sins no more. Isn't it wonderful that My Father blots out your sins when you ask and remember them no more? Each of you remembers the sins of family, friends, peers, and colleagues and sometimes reminds them of their sins. The listed individuals can be church members. As humans, forgiveness is challenging, but it must be done to reach heaven. Blessed is the person whose sins are forgiven. A burden is lifted off them, and you also when you forgive others. When you ask for forgiveness, My death covered your sins, and they are blotted out. Only I can blot out your transgressions. Enjoy the tranquility that accompanies forgiveness.
Peace and blessings.

Peace And Blessings : with the Risen *SON*

Day
Two Hundred and Seventy Nine

Your Challenge

Romans 3:23 (KJV): "For all have sinned and come short of the glory of God;" Everyone has sinned. Therefore, I have a challenge for you. If you decide to accept it, your challenge is to select a four-hour block of time (8-12, 12- 4, or 4-8) and live without doing a known sin. No sinning in your words, actions, deeds, and thoughts. Before your block of time has expired, you will call on me several times, asking for forgiveness. My Father sent Me to be the sacrificial lamb because He knew you would sin and break your relationship with Him. When you sin, ask for forgiveness, and I will forgive you so your relationship with My Father can be restored. Accepting this challenge will teach you of Me (Jesus) and the Holy Spirit. *Peace and blessings.*

Day
Two Hundred and Eighty

Getting Up

"But if we confess our sins, he is faithful and righteous, forgiving us our sins and cleansing us from all unrighteousness." John 1:9 (NET)

Getting up from a sinful situation is challenging. Pride, embarrassment, and shame kick in, and you find yourself like Adam and Eve, hiding from Me. You cannot sew enough fig leaves together to hide what you have done. Get out of your sin, ask for forgiveness, grace, and mercy, and face the consequences of your past actions. When you fall physically, use three contact points to get up (left hand, right hand, and one leg). When you fall spiritually, use three points of contact to get up (Me, Jesus, My Father, and the Holy Spirit). Ask forgiveness for anyone else involved and work on rebuilding the trust in that relationship. Note: Rebuilding trust is not an overnight process. As you progress, do not become a repeat offender. Learn from your past mistakes (sins). Hold my hand as you move forward, and I will help you not to stumble or fall. ***Peace and blessings.***

Peace And Blessings : with the Risen *SON*

Day
Two Hundred and Eighty One

Forgive, Forgive, and Forgive

Have you ever taken a serious look at defining forgiveness?
It means to stop feeling angry or resentful toward (someone)
for an offense, flaw, mistake, or sin. Some people do not
want to forgive others. Their goal is to punish them. I did
not give them the right to punish another person. How long
do you punish a person, one day, a week, a month, or years?
Some can only forgive a person one time. As you know,
those individuals do not have many friends. Real forgiveness
is to stop being resentful or angry and to show forgetfulness
by not talking about the incident. When an individual
asks for forgiveness, the individual is forgiven. All this
time, you think you are punishing the individual, but you
are punishing yourself because the individual was released
by Me when they asked for forgiveness. Stop punishing
yourself and learn to forgive. Families forgive, spouses
forgive, children forgive, Christians forgive, leaders forgive,
individuals forgive, and you forgive.

"And forgive us our sins, as we have forgiven those who sin
against us." Matthew 6:12 (NLT) I forgave you when you
asked, why can't you forgive others? ***Peace and blessings.***

Peace And Blessings : with the Risen *SON*

Day
Two Hundred and Eighty Two

Personal Sin

"Sin is portrayed in scripture as falling short of God's glory, going astray like a wandering sheep, transgressing or overstepping the law, and trespassing, which means exercising your own will in the realm of divine authority.

Sin brings hideous results, not only affecting your relationship with Me but also your relationship with others. Sin is a three-letter word that brings major consequences in this life and your eternal destination. All have sinned and fallen short of the glory of God. Yes, I gave my life as a ransom to redeem you from the devil's grasp and control, and you are no longer one of his pawns. Your salvation was purchased with My life. Daily, you must address your status and ask for forgiveness if required. If you think you are sinless, you are deceiving yourself. Do not allow pride to get in the way of your salvation. Hold my hand and allow the Holy Spirit and Me to guide you.
Peace and blessings.

Peace And Blessings : with the Risen *SON*

Day
Two Hundred and Eighty Three

If You Fall

2 Samuel 11 best illustrates an individual falling in sin. David was told Bathsheba was the daughter of Eliam, the wife of Uriah the Hittite, one of his soldiers. King David sent for Bathsheba, made love to her, and then sent her home. Bathsheba sent word to David that she was pregnant. David sent word to his general to put Bathsheba's husband in the thick of the battle. He even went as far to command him to withdraw, so he could die in the battle. One sin leads to another to cover what he had done.

When you sin, do not do like David and try to prevent exposure (what is done in the dark ALWAYS comes to light). Don't pull an Adam and Eve and try to hide from Me. There is no place you can hide from Me. While you were sinning, I was looking right at you! Yes, I saw EVERY choice you made. I even gave you an opportunity to acknowledge what you have done and repent. But you allowed yourself to be influenced by Satan himself. He gave you all the excuses types of reasons to avoid seeking forgiveness. But I challenge you that if you fall into sin and you will, get up as quickly. The longer you wait, the harder it is to course correct. Ask Me and the person you have offended for forgiveness. If they choose not to forgive you, do not worry. You have done your part. Now, once I have forgiven you, work hard not to become a repeat offender. Now get up and walk closer to me. ***Peace and blessings.***

Peace And Blessings : with the Risen *SON*

Day
Two Hundred and Eighty Four

Do Something Different Today

"For all have sinned and come short of the glory of God;"
Romans 3:23 (KJV)

I am challenging you to not knowingly to sin all day. Do not do anything that you know is a sin. I am challenging you to do what you are supposed to do anyway, not sin. Do unto others as you would want them to do unto you. When you put this thought process into play, you are working to be kind, fair, and loving to everyone. Treat others the same way I have been treating you. If you fall short of this goal, ask for forgiveness, and start over again. If the Holy Spirit shows you a sin that you were committing, ask for forgiveness, change what you were doing, and do not become a repeat offender. You are building your relationship with Me and others by trying not to sin. My challenge is for you not to sin; you can do it if you walk very close to me. Move forward with this challenge.
Peace and blessings.

Peace And Blessings : with the Risen *SON*

Day
Two Hundred and Eighty Five

A Clean Slate

"As far as the east is from the west, so far has he removed our transgressions from us." Psalms 103:12 (NIV)

You hear these words often when people are dealing with forgiveness. Let's unpack it. North and South have designated positions: North Pole and South Pole. You are headed south regardless of which direction you leave the North Pole. You are headed north regardless of which direction you leave the South Pole. East and West are different. When headed west, you can travel worldwide and never meet East. You may be north or south of the equator but still traveling in the same direction. East and West can never meet like the North Pole and South Pole. Therefore, as far as the East is from the West, I have removed your transgressions. This is what I have done for you. Once forgiven, all your old sins are thrown away. You are given a clean slate, a fresh start! Pay it forward by extending grace to others and give them the same thing you have been given, a clean slate.

I challenge you to forgive quicker, even if others do not ask. Forgiveness relieves your stress and allows you to let Me, CHRIST (the world's light) shine in you. This light is like a beacon on a hill, leading others to me as you shine like a beacon on a hill, leading others to Me. *Peace and blessings.*

Peace And Blessings : with the Risen *SON*

Day
Two Hundred and Eighty Six

Forgiving Yourself

"But if we confess our sins to him, he is faithful and just to forgive us our sins and to cleanse us from all wickedness." 1 John 1:9

Forgiving yourself is a tremendous part of the repentance process. Do not allow Satan to control your mind with negative thoughts about Me. I, died on the cross for your sins. No human was worthy or sinless; therefore, My Father sent me to be your sacrificial lamb to die a very painful death. When you join Me at the cross, you understand forgiveness better and My Father's love for you. Your task is to ask for forgiveness. Once God has forgiven you for your sins, He has removed them as far as the East is from the West. If you love yourself, forgive yourself, and stop holding yourself hostage and under Satan's control. Hold My hand, walk with Me, and allow Me to insert peace, tranquility, comfort, grace, mercy, and love in your life as we build or restore a wonderful relationship. ***Peace and blessings.***

Peace And Blessings : with the Risen *SON*

Day
Two Hundred and Eighty Seven

Pray for Your Enemies

"You have heard the law that says, love your neighbor and hate your enemies. But I say, love your enemies! Pray for those who persecute you!" Matthew 5:43-44 (NLT)

It sounds so crazy to pray for your enemies and those who are against you. There will always be individuals who are against you. Throughout My ministry, I had enemies. Surely, you should not expect less. But the word is to love and be nice and kind to them. You show the love I taught you to love others as I have loved you. Greater is he that is in you than in the world. The Comforter should be in you, guiding, teaching, and allowing you to do great things. You must be counterintuitive and do the unexpected by praying for those who dislike you, hate you, or even have desires to kill you. Killing them with kindness allows Me to draw them unto Me. Do as I have commanded you, and I will take care of the rest. *Peace and blessings.*

Day
Two Hundred and Eighty Eight

Reboot

"For all have sinned and come short of the glory of God." Romans 3:23 (KJV)

A restart/reboot is a single step involving both shutting down and powering on something. A reboot is an act or instance of booting a computer system again. When you restart a phone, everything in your RAM is cleared out, purging fragments of previously running apps and closing any open apps. Every time you ask for forgiveness, you reboot or give your soul a fresh start. Do you realize how many times per day you reboot? Some of you may go for an hour while others every five minutes. I forgive you and give you a fresh start each time you ask to reboot. You are purged, cleaned, and the fragments of the previous sins are removed.

Be careful to not practice sin! What does that mean? To not change and be a person who apologizes in word but not in action. But if you fall again, reboot and get up quickly. I will never leave or forsake you. Hold my hand as you continue your journey. ***Peace and blessings.***

Peace And Blessings : with the Risen *SON*

Temptation

Day
Two Hundred and Eighty Nine

Facing Temptation

It is not a matter of if you will encounter temptation, but when. You will face temptations until you reach eternal glory. Remember, though I had one Son without sin, I have never had one without temptation. Consider this when you fast: food becomes the first thing you seek once your fast ends. Always pray before you break your fast. When Satan tried to tempt Me in the wilderness, suggesting I turn stones into bread to satisfy My hunger, I countered his ploy with Scripture: 'Man shall not live by bread alone, but by every word that proceeds from the mouth of God.' This teaches you, too, that when tempted—whether by Satan or others—to defend yourself or react impulsively, respond with Scripture. To effectively wield this weapon, you must know it well. Whenever you face temptation, remember that I am always with you, ready to help you overcome.

Remember when the tempter came to Me and said, 'If You are the Son of God, command that these stones become bread.' Matthew 4:3 (NKJV)
Peace and blessings.

Peace And Blessings : with the Risen *SON*

Day Two Hundred and Ninety

Temptation Part 2

Temptation is the desire to do something wrong or unwise. Temptation is a thing or course of action that attracts or tempts someone. "It is written again; Thou shalt not tempt the Lord thy God" is what I told Satan when he asked me to jump from a high location. I could jump off a high place, and my Father would command angels to catch me. But to do so would be testing my Father. Tempting, in this case, is the testing. Tempt means to put to the test, to prove out, to try, or to test My patience. I allow you to test Me with tithes and offerings. The purpose of this test is to bless you if you are sincere and a cheerful giver. Test my Father in the areas he provides for you to test Him, but do not tempt Him to try to prove a point because it could be costly.
Peace and blessings.

Peace And Blessings : with the Risen *SON*

Day
Two Hundred and Ninety One

Temptation Part 3

Satan asked me to bow to him, and he would give me
the world's kingdoms. Wow, what a generous offer.
'Satan makes you a generous offer also. Note to
yourself: Satan is only offering you what you already
have. As my disciples, I have everything that you need.
Satan tempts and entices you to make you feel like
what I have for you is insufficient. You have heard the
saying, "If you let Satan ride, he will want to drive."
Do not bow to Satan in any form or fashion, in words,
deeds, or actions. Satan attacks where he thinks you are
weak. But you can do everything through Me, Christ,
which strengthens you.

Be strong, be courageous because I am with you.
"Away from me, Satan! For it is written: Worship the
Lord your God and serve him only." Matthew 4:10
(NIV) *Peace and blessings.*

Peace And Blessings : with the Risen *SON*

Day
Two Hundred and Ninety Two

When Your Flesh Calls

I define the flesh as the earthly part of man that tells the mind I am hungry. The spiritual man fights the urges that the worldly man is requesting. The human taste buds call for something sweet to eat. You know you should not have it because you have diabetes, but the urge is so strong that you give the flesh what it requests. What happens when the flesh is calling for sinful things? How do you fight it when your lust for something is overwhelming? When you first felt the urge, you should have called on me to help you fight Satan, and these desires were placed in the forefront of your mind. I can help you fight the lust of the flesh, the lust of the eye, and the pride of life. You are not the only person fighting these desires or calling on me for help.

Trust Me, when you call, help is on the way. I will not leave or forsake you. I will give you an avenue or path so you can escape. Do not think about it; take it and renew and refresh our relationship with me, and I will bless you abundantly. There hath no temptation taken you, but such as is common to man: but God is faithful, who will not suffer you to be tempted above that ye are able; but will with the temptation also make a way to escape, that ye may be able to bear it.
Peace and blessings.

Peace And Blessings : with the Risen *SON*

Day
Two Hundred and Ninety Three

Through it All, I Love You

One definition of through is to continue in time toward the completion of a process or period. I warned Peter of Satan's desire to sift him and the other disciples like wheat. "Satan desired to sift them by his temptations and endeavored by those troubles to draw them into sin, to put them into a loss and hurry, as corn when it is sifted to bring the chaff uppermost, or rather to shake out the wheat and leave nothing but the chaff." (Matthew Henry Commentary) Shortly after this, Peter denied knowing me three times.

While Peter was going through these trying times, I still loved him. As you are going through COVID-19, job issues, family problems, financial situations, car problems, church issues, neighborhood challenges, and homeowners' associations, to name a few things, I have not left or forsaken you because I love you. Fear not, trust, and have faith in me; I will bring you through the completion of these challenges. Remain faithful.
Peace and blessings.

Peace And Blessings : with the Risen *SON*

Day
Two Hundred and Ninety Four

The Road Less Traveled

The road called life presents many opportunities for humankind.
Yes, we make choices daily to do whatever we want. Having a
choice is terrific, especially when it is a favorable choice. But
there are instances where we make bad choices. Nevertheless, I
will give you that opportunity. Today, I am presenting you with
a chance to travel to a road with a Y intersection. The road to
the left is well-traveled and much more comprehensive than the
road on the right. The road on the right has minimal signs of
travel and is narrow. Few people encourage you to turn around
or get off the broad road. When on the road called straight, all
your harmful friends call you and encourage you to get off and
follow them. Once off, it becomes seven times harder to get
back on the road called straight because seven other evil spirits
are attacking you. As you look at society today, so many are on
the broad, wide road and having an enjoyable time with Satan.
Do not be afraid to travel the narrow road; you are not alone;
God is there with you. Is the life you are living good to you or
suitable for you? Hey, there are people on the narrow road.

"Enter through the narrow gate, for wide is the gate that leads
to destruction, and many enter through it. But small is the gate
and narrow the road that leads to life, and only a few find it."
Matthew 7:13-14 *Peace and blessings.*

Peace And Blessings : with the Risen *SON*

Day
Two Hundred and Ninety Five

Use Your Words

There will be times when you are faced with major
opportunities that make falling into temptation easy. I challenge
you to use one of the most powerful weapons I have given you,
your words. Life and death are in the power of your tongue.
You can bind and loose and watch things happen. So, when
the enemy tempts you, silence him with your words! Today,
remember you have been given a weapon that can create and
destroy the works of the enemy; don't be afraid to use it.
Peace and Blessings.

Peace And Blessings : with the Risen *SON*

Day
Two Hundred and Ninety Six

4th Word from the Cross

I am on the cross in pain, suffering from my wounds, and suddenly, the earth becomes dark. The weight of all the people's sins is on me—those before, those in the present, and those in the future. I am the world's light; now my Father shows me darkness. Darkness represents sin, and now the sin of humanity is upon me, and my Father appears to have turned his back on me, and for the first time, we are separated. When you sin, you become separated from Me. I never sinned but carried and suffered for your sins. Do not allow this pain and agony to be in vain because you will not forgive or stop sinning. Change what you are doing while there is time. Repent and restore your relationship with God the Father. You never want to be separated from My Father because it is a dark world without Him. My God, why have you forsaken me? "Matthew 27:46 (KJV)
Peace and blessings.

Peace And Blessings : with the Risen *SON*

Day
Two Hundred and Ninety Seven

Spiritual Spring Cleaning

When you were growing up, your mother conducted spring cleaning of your house on a warm spring day. On that day, no one could leave the yard. You had to be available and ready to run to your mother when she called. The beds were broken down, the mattress was taken out and placed in the sun, the bed springs were washed, everything was taken out of the rooms, and the rooms were cleaned from top to bottom. During this process, things not used or needed were thrown away. Spring cleaning a house is much easier than spring cleaning one spirituality. Mentally, you feel you are okay or good to go. But when you realize you are not perfect and identify items in your life that cause you to fall short of perfection, those are the items you must throw out. Ask me to wash the items you need to keep and to assist in identifying what to throw out because one does not want to let go of various items (sins). Do you remember the fresh scent of the house once it was cleaned? Nothing can compare to the smell of a spiritually cleansed soul. ***Peace and blessings.***

Peace And Blessings : with the Risen *SON*

Day
Two Hundred and Ninety Eight

I'm on the Right Road Now

As you travel down the heavenly-bound road, stay focused on your mission. There will be lots of invitations to get off the road. Pay no attention to the cat calls. People will say you can do what they are doing and get back on the road. Hmmm, why have they not gotten back on? Do not be fooled into thinking you can conquer your thorn and return on the heavenly-bound road. Look at drug users; most are hooked for life, and only a few escape. Do not gamble with your soul; you only get one.

I have enough adventures for you to keep the excitement in your life. Ask, and it shall be given; seek, and you shall find it. Stay on the road and enjoy the benefits of My sheep. When invited to get off the road, say Baaa, like a sheep. "Enter through the narrow gate. For wide is the gate and broad is the road that leads to destruction, and many enter through it." Matthew 7:13 (NIV) *Peace and blessings.*

Peace And Blessings : with the Risen *SON*

Day
Two Hundred and Ninety Nine

A Thorn in Your Side

II Corinthians 12:7-8 discusses that the Apostle Paul had a thorn in his side. He asked the Lord three times to remove it, but God would not. The Bible does not actually state what Paul's thorn was. We speculate or guess it was an illness of his body or a vice, but nonetheless, it made Paul request God for relief, but God denied his request. Each of you has a thorn in our side or vice that haunts us. Do you allow your thorn or vice to control you? Do you know what your thorn is? Do you call on Me for relief or try to get through it yourself? You need to know your limitations and ask Me for assistance. As much as you and I know your vise, so does Satan.

Satan kicks very strongly when God is about to bless you by agitating you with your thorn. Do not give in to Satan; call on Me, Jesus, to assist you. Don't be ashamed; you are not the only one with a thorn. Hold out and enjoy the blessing I have for you.
Peace and blessings.

Peace And Blessings : with the Risen *SON*

Day
Three Hundred

Avoid Temptations

Temptations, temptations, and more temptations. Life has many temptations, whether someone presents them to you, or you find them on your own. The beautiful thing is that I am there to bring you through. If you stick close to me, I will show you how to escape. If you do unto others as you would have them do unto you, do not tempt them. Do not tempt a person to sin in all the things you may do. Convince them not to sin and do all you can to move them from sin. You should understand this better since you were tempted. Temptations come in many forms, places, and people. Do not be surprised at what temptation looks like. You know your weaknesses, so run from them through the path I show you. Satan tempted me, and you will be too. Use scripture to defeat him and get out of the area. Do not give in, and I will bless you. "There will always be temptations to sin, but what sorrow awaits the person who does the tempting!" Luke 17:1 (NLT)
Peace and blessings.

 Peace And Blessings : with the Risen *SON*

Day
Three Hundred and One

Peace be Still

In life, we face many storms or challenging situations. It is how you handle adversity that makes the difference in your recovery. The disciples were no different than you. I was with them on the ship, but they still feared the storm destroying it. During your storm, you can tell yourself, "Peace be still," and quieted the storm, winds, and waves of fear because I am with you. Now is the time to tell Me, who already knows what you are going through and what you need or want. Be specific about your desired outcome. Call on Me for relief, plant your mustard seed, and watch your tiny seed become a tree of faith. "And he arose, and rebuked the wind, and said unto the sea, Peace, be still. And the wind ceased, and there was a great calm. And he said unto them, why are ye so fearful? how is it that ye have no faith?"
Mark 4:39-40 *Peace and blessings.*

Peace And Blessings : with the Risen *SON*

Day
Three Hundred and Two

Retrograde to Move Forward

Retrograde means reverting to an earlier and inferior condition or position as directed or moved backward. Regardless of the title, regress, retreat, fallback, released, fired, or retrograde, one must return to a former life position. Your human instincts feel hurt and pain, as well as your feeling being used by others. God can direct you to a former position, location, or place in time to get you out of danger, to get your attention, to equip, prepare, or organize you to move forward to a position of greater responsibility. Take a positive outlook and attitude since you have no control over this, but the God you worship and serve does. God makes the things people do to harm you to your advantage and His glory. Do your part by updating your resume, looking for employment, and trusting God. Be on guard as God opens the windows of heaven and pours out blessings just for you. Continue to hold God's hand and walk with Him. *Peace and blessings.*

Peace And Blessings : with the Risen *SON*

Day
Three Hundred and Three

God Knows Your Heart

I came to Cain after he presented his offering, which I did not accept. Although Cain's offering was not blood, it could have been better. Cain is mad or upset and plans what to do to his brother Abel. I knew Cain's intention and addressed Cain." Your facial expression has changed; let go of whatever is on your mind. Satan is at your door (working on your mind) to encourage you to sin, but you must overrule Satan." Just as I knew Cain's innermost thoughts, I know yours. It is important to understand that to ascend to My hill, your heart must be pure, and your hands must be clean.
Peace and blessings.

Peace And Blessings : with the Risen *SON*

Day
Three Hundred and Four

Be Angry, but Don't Sin

In your anger do not sin": Wrath or anger is a human emotion we must live with. Paul instructs on being angry; it is okay, but do not allow yourself to fall into sin.

Anger encouraged Cain to kill his brother Abel. Anger can cause you to say things you will regret the next day. When overcome by anger, that part of you have been suppressing can become uncontrollable. Do not allow individuals to push your anger button(s). When angered, seek a resolution before the setting of the sun. Peaceful resolutions allow you to have a restful night, and anger does not brew throughout the night. The Holy Spirit is there to help you through this trying moment. What have you got to lose? Talk to God, your creator, friend, and savior, to give you deliverance. God can and will deliver you; ask and see for yourself. Ephesians 4:26 "Be ye angry, and sin not: let not the sun go down upon your wrath: (KJV) Do not let the sun go down while you are still angry, (NIV)." **_Peace and blessings._**

Peace And Blessings : with the Risen *SON*

Day
Three Hundred and Five

When you Have Storms

As we rest in the storm, be calm, have assurance, and know this storm is in your favor. Sometimes, you do not slow down and become sick, but God has a way of caring for his disciples. The snow (which cleans the air) and ice (kills the bugs in the ground and balances nature) are good for us and allow us to get more rest, and in most cases, our jobs give us time off with pay. "Isn't God good?" There may be a storm in someone's life. Regardless of the type of storm (hurricane or tornado) or the size of the storm, there is a God, a Savior, and a sweet, merciful Jesus who can calm any storm. Are you willing to let Jesus calm your life's storm(s)? Call on Me and tell Me about your situation; ask Me to bless the one who initiated the storm and thank Him for the storm. If the storm had not come, would you be talking to Me?

Meditate and contemplate on Me. "And he saith unto them, why are ye fearful, O ye of little faith? Then he arose and rebuked the winds and the sea, and there was a great calm." Matthew 8:26 (KJV)
Peace and blessings.

Peace And Blessings : with the Risen *SON*

Day
Three Hundred and Six

Rumors

Rumor has it that the next President of the United States will initiate a war. In life, you will hear of rumors and wars. Do not chase rumors, especially if they are about you. You will never catch or stop them. You will hear of predictions and individuals claiming to be Me, Jesus. Have no fear. I am still in control and have informed My disciples to be alert, beware, and pay attention to false information. In times like these, you must stay focused, continue to pray, read, and study to keep our spiritual vision on point. God, your creator, will lead and guide you to the truth. "For many shall come in my name, saying, I am Christ; and shall deceive many. And ye shall hear of wars and rumors of wars: see that ye be not troubled: for all these things must come to pass, but the end is not yet." Matthew 24:5 (KJV)
Peace and blessings.

Peace And Blessings : with the Risen *SON*

Day
Three Hundred and Seven

Blessed is the Man

What is life without challenges, boring? Nobody wants to go through temptation because it is a spiritual battle. Satan challenged Me when I came out of the wilderness from a forty-day fast, offering Me what I already had. Satan tempts humankind by making offers of things you already have to steal your souls with false promises. Temptation is something you must endure as I did. James says, "Blessed is the man that endures the temptation." You endure temptation by calling on Me to help you overcome it because Satan attacks your weakness and at your weakness moment. Because you love God, you do not want to disappoint God; therefore, you call on God to deliver you to enjoy the crown of life at the end of this life. You are living this life in Christ to live again with Christ. "Blessed is the man that endured temptation: for when he is tried, he shall receive the crown of life, which the Lord hath promised to them that love him." James 1:12 (KJV)
Peace and blessings.

Peace And Blessings : with the Risen *SON*

Day
Three Hundred and Eight

Presenting You Faultless

Jude, the brother of James, speaks about salvation through Jesus. I am the one who can keep you from falling if you depend on Me. If you try to do things independently, you will fail and fall. When Peter focused on Me, Jesus, Peter walked on water. Just like Peter, you fall when you lose your focus on your savior. I can keep you from falling if you trust in Me. And even better, I will present you faultless, that is, without blame, in the splendor and bliss of heaven, the final home where you want to spend eternity. What do you need to do to stay focused on Me? Do not allow Satan to draw you into sin or to make you fall short of God's glorious, endless life He is willing to give you. Thank you, Jesus, for presenting us faultless. Now unto him who is able to keep you from falling, and to present you faultless before the presence of his glory with exceeding joy Jude 1:24 (NIV) *Peace and blessings.*

Peace And Blessings : with the Risen *SON*

Day
Three Hundred and Nine

Hot as Hell

There are various colors to define heat or fire. The color is due to the heat of the fire and what it is burning. Relatively cool fires burn red, orange, yellow, green, blue, indigo, and violet as the fire gets hotter. Our eyes see this violet as a white color. How hot is hell or the Lake of Fire? Do you want to know? Humanity cannot define or know the degree of heat that hell emits or produces. The Bible does not give a definitive description of how hot the lake of fire is. Disciples work to ensure your name is in the lamb's book of life. There is time to repent, to turn 180 degrees (turn around), and to walk with and for Christ. Eternal life is beyond what this world can offer because it is out of this world. And whosoever was not found written in the book of life was cast into the lake of fire." Revelation 20:15 (KJV)
Peace and blessings.

Day
Three Hundred and Ten

Go and Sin No More

I encountered a man who had been waiting thirty-eight years to enter a pool after an angel touched the water. Someone always entered before him and received healing. I told him to take up his bed and walk; it was a sabbath day. Pharisees and other leaders inquired of him carrying his bed on a sabbath day, and he told his story. Later, I saw this man in the temple and told him he was made well, sin no more, or something worse would happen to him. Do you know you must work diligently to sin no more when healed? You are impotent to some degree and need or require Me to lift you in forgiveness so you can enjoy a healthy and quality spiritual life. As I have blessed and healed you, "Go and sin no more." "Then they asked him, "Who is the Man who said to you, 'Take up your bed and walk'?" But the one who was healed did not know who it was, for I had withdrawn, a multitude being in that place. Afterward, I found him in the temple and said, "See, you have been made well. Sin no more, lest a worse thing come upon you." John 5:12- 14 (NIV) *Peace and blessings.*

Peace And Blessings : with the Risen *SON*

Day
Three Hundred and Eleven

Take My Yoke

For some strange reason, humans place burdens on themselves. I call this self-inflicted. Nevertheless, I invite you to take My yoke, learn of Me, and find rest for your souls. A yoke is built for two; therefore, when you take My yoke, your load is lightened because I AM carrying it.

I take away the world's pressures because you are connected to Me. You are learning more about Me. I AM connected to the Father. His yoke has a heavenly connection, and the rest, He invites you to be spiritual. Because you are now connected to Him, I can fight your spiritual battles, thus giving you a lighter load. You are now at the altar; give Me your burdens and let Me carry them for you. I say my yoke is easy, and my burdens are light. Hook up to Me 'yoke, relax, and allow Me to carry your sickness, pains, finances, family, problems in your job and much more. Once you connect your burdens and problems to My yoke, if you take your burdens back, your burdens are self-inflicted. "Take my yoke on you and learn from me, because I am gentle and humble in heart, and you will find rest for your souls. For my yoke is easy to bear, and my load is not hard to carry."
Matthew 11:29-30 (NIV) *Peace and blessings.*

Peace And Blessings : with the Risen *SON*

Day
Three Hundred and Twelve

In the Way

Saul sought to capture all the Christians (which
the religious leaders called "in the way"). Saul was
traveling to Damascus seeking those "in the way." Still,
he was traveling the wrong way, away from Jerusalem.
While going to Damascus, Saul encountered a bright
light and fell from his mule, blinded by the light. I
told Saul that he was "in the way" and to stop kicking
against the prick.

I instructed Saul to continue to Damascus to a specific
location. Now Saul, one who was traveling the wrong
way, seeking those in the way, was told to get out of the
way and was sent to see Simon, who was in the way of
converting Saul to the way. How would I see you today;
"in the way" or in the way? If you are in My way, get
out of the way and follow Me "in the way." And desired
of him letters to Damascus to the synagogues, that if he
found any of this way, whether they were men or
women, he might bring them bound unto Jerusalem.
Acts 9:2 (KJV)" *Peace and blessings.*

Peace And Blessings : with the Risen *SON*

Day
Three Hundred and Thirteen

Get Your Spiritual System Checked

Daily, hourly, and every minute, the Holy Spirit
conducts a scan of you and reminds you of old viruses
or sinful things trying to penetrate your spiritual wall of
defense. Where are you in this process? Do you allow
the Holy Spirit to defend you from old viruses that can
cause you to regress or return to your old sinful world?
The virus could be a person, place, or thing. Protection
is available; you do not have to click a mouse; follow
the Holy Spirit's guidance as you are led in the right
direction in your words, actions, deeds, and thoughts.
When the Holy Spirit wants to check you for sins, let
the Holy Spirit have its way and enjoy a virus-free life.
Upgrades are not required because, with Me, sin is sin.
Peace and blessings.

Peace And Blessings : with the Risen *SON*

Day
Three Hundred and Fourteen

Taking Ownership

"Whoever conceals their sins does not prosper, but the one who confesses and renounces them finds mercy."
Proverbs 28:13 (NIV)

Have you met individuals who never take responsibility for their wrong actions or words? They give excuses as to why it is not their fault or responsibility. A sincere, humble, or upright person takes responsibility for their impropriety or wrongness to mend or rebuild relationships. When an individual takes responsibility for their actions or words, that individual becomes a better person and gains the respect of family, friends, and colleagues. What about you? Do you take ownership of your improprieties? If you want to be blessed, be the homeowner of your mistakes or sins. I will be with you so do not feel alone as you walk closer to and with me. *Peace and blessings.*

Peace And Blessings : with the Risen *SON*

Day
Three Hundred and Fifteen

Gaslighting

Gaslighting is someone using psychological methods to make a person question their sanity or reasoning powers. The serpent tells Eve about My instructions to Adam regarding the forbidden fruit. The serpent aroused Eve's interest and desire to taste the forbidden fruit. Adam, on the other hand, did not speak up and correct the serpent.

Be aware of individuals gaslighting you and trying to make you question your feelings, thinking, and reasoning ability. Do not be surprised who will use gaslighting against you. Know the instructions and sticking with the plan as Noah did with the ark. I will not leave or forsake you in need; call on me. "And the serpent said unto the woman, Ye shall not surely die: For God doth know that in the day ye eat thereof, then your eyes shall be opened, and ye shall be as gods, knowing good and evil." Genesis 3:4-5 (KJV)
Peace and blessings.

Peace And Blessings : with the Risen *SON*

Day
Three Hundred and Sixteen

When the Benediction is Over

The Benediction Prayer is a short and beautiful prayer set in poetic form. It begins with the words, "May the Lord bless you and keep you." What do you do when worship is completed, and the benediction is given? Do you "Go ye therefore, and teach all nations, baptizing them in the name of the Father, and of the Son, and of the Holy Ghost?" When you walk out of the church, did the message refresh you, did it reform you, did it empower you or cause a change in your relationship with Me; did you follow the Holy Spirit's guidance, or did you revert to who you were before you entered the church? The benediction says to bless and keep you. Did you get the blessing, or did the blessing bypass you because you did not have My blood on the doorpost of your heart? You did not make me the center of your joy; therefore, you missed your blessing(s). If so, you are missing many blessings because I know your heart. When the benediction is over, Satan will test you to see how much power he gained or lost. Stay focused on Me, and I will keep you and make your battle my battle. After the benediction, stay focused on Me as you continue your journey. ***Peace and blessings.***

Peace And Blessings : with the Risen *SON*

Day
Three Hundred and Seventeen

Wiles Of The Devil

"Put on the full armor of God, so that you can take your stand against the devil's schemes." Ephesians 6:11 (NIV)

Wiles are tricks or manipulations designed to deceive someone. Wiles of the devil are those clever schemes used by Satan to ensnare you through temptation, threat, or intimidation." Satan uses any tool necessary to tempt or persuade you to seek and enjoy sinful things. Because you are in a war with Satan, I equipped you with armor for your battlefield. Read Ephesians 6: 13-18 (KJV) to pick up your battlefield armor. I can be your armor bearer because of the many battles you will encounter. There is no armor for your back because you never turn your back to the enemy. I will not leave or forsake, follow the guidance of the Holy Spirit, and attack your enemy. Weak, complacent individuals are considered soft, easy targets. Do not wait for Satan to attack you because your best defense is a solid offense to keep Satan running from you. *Peace and blessings.*

Peace And Blessings : with the Risen *SON*

Day
Three Hundred and Eighteen

The Cost of Sin

A sin is an immoral act against a divine directive. Sin is humanity going against God's rules, plans, commands, and directives. KJV) Romans 3:23: "For all have sinned and come short of the glory of God." Sin is very costly. Sin takes you where you do not want to go. It keeps you longer than you want to stay. Sin costs you more than you want to pay. Sin will make you lie to cover up what you did, so man will not know, but I do. Sin greatly offends Me. When you sin, you deserve the death penalty. When you sin, you grieve the Holy Spirit. When you sin, you suspend the exercise of your faith. Sin severely wounds your conscience. When you sin, you break relationships. When sin leaves a crimson stain (a bloody mess), call on me for forgiveness, and I can wash you white as snow.

Work hard not to become a repeat offender. Everyone sins; the difference between individuals is how quickly one recovers, renews, or refreshes their relationship with me. Now that you know the cost of sin, do not sin so you do not have to pay the heavy price. Walk closer with me so you can avoid all the problems that await your company. Try not to sin and have an enjoyable day. Hold my hand so you do not stumble or fall. *Peace and blessings.*

Peace And Blessings : with the Risen *SON*

Day
Three Hundred and Nineteen

You Talk too Much

James 3:5 (KJV) says, "Even so the tongue is a little member, and boasteth great things. Behold, how great a matter a little fire kindleth!" Do you realize how much you talk about things you have no or partial information about? If you need something to talk about, tell the story of my last week in Jerusalem as I went to the cross. It's a true event that will spark conversations. Tell others I was crucified and how it became dark at mid day. Don't forget to tell them I was put in a borrowed tomb, but on the third day, I rose and gave the tomb back to the owner. Please tell them that I am their priest now if you must tell it. Tell them I died for their sins only because I love them. Accept My assistance in controlling your words, and your actions will follow.
Peace and blessings.

Day
Three Hundred and Twenty

Color Coded Sins

Proverbs list the seven deadly sins in chapter 6:16-19. Below, they are color-coded. Does your favorite color match your possible deadly sin? Green envy is best described as a desire for something more and to covet other people's belongings and status. The opposite of envy is love. Violet pride is when a person feels more special or important than others. At its worst, pride is narcissism (self-centered). The opposite of pride is humility. Red-Wrath can be best described as anger or hatred. It is the opposite of kindness. Light Blue -Sloth is the act of being lazy or idle. The opposite of sloth is zeal — or eagerness to achieve something good. Blue-Lust is the act of giving into desire. The opposite of lust is self- control. Yellow greed is the desire for wealth and status. The opposite of greed is generosity. Orange-Gluttony is the act of consuming more than you need. The opposite of gluttony is temperance — being disciplined and wise with resources. Connect with Me and the Holy Spirit to assist you in avoiding these deadly sins. ***Peace and blessings.***

Peace And Blessings : with the Risen *SON*

Day
Three Hundred and Twenty One

Can You Work Without A Title?

Distinguishing individuals by religious titles is widespread in the world. You see and hear many people addressed today as Doctor, Reverend, Pastor, Father, Elder, Bishops, Deacons, Trustees, and many more. Do you need a title before your name or initials after your name to be a Christian, i.e., the Reverend Doctor, or the initials BA, MDiv, or DMin? Even though Paul was and is probably the most influential apostle in the church's history, he writes with humility. How effective were you before the titles? I called you to be an example before you were in your mother's womb. What has changed other than you becoming aware of titles? When you come face-to-face with Me in judgment, I will not call you by title but by your name. I will not call groups, i.e., The Alpha Men, the Q Dogs, Alpha Kappa Alpha, Morning Star Church, or Oberlin Road Baptist Church, just everyone by name. A title does not make you the person you want to be. It shows you received additional training. Can you work for me without a title? I hope that you can. Untitled yourself and use the title I gave you, CHRISTIAN. ***Peace and blessings.***

Peace And Blessings : with the Risen *SON*

Day
Three Hundred and Twenty Two

Spiritual SOS

"In my distress I called to the Lord; I cried to my God for help. From his temple, he heard my voice; my cry came before him, into his ears." Psalm 18:6 (NIV)

"SOS" (Save Our Souls) is the International Morse code distress signal. The Morse code machine uses three short taps for an S, three long taps for an O, and three short taps for another S. Anyone receiving this signal knows a person is in distress. I know Morse code, all the languages, and so much more. David says in his distress, I call on the Lord. He did not mention Morse code as his method of contacting the Lord but just called on Him, and God heard David's call. You can call on Me just like David did, and I will listen. If you are troubled, in disarray, unsure of yourself, or need to talk to Me, call on Me, and I will answer. ***Peace and blessings.***

Peace And Blessings : with the Risen *SON*

Day
Three Hundred and Twenty Three

Don't Let Green Grass Fool You

"You say the grass is always greener on the other side of the fence? You mean that other people often seem to be in a better situation than you, but their situation may not be as good as it seems. You know what it's like, the grass is always greener on the other side of the fence. I always look at jobs advertised online and think I'd be better off elsewhere. Grass and greener are often used in other expressions with a similar meaning. Many players who left in the past found that the grass isn't always greener elsewhere. You cannot have your staff believing that the grass is always greener in another company." If you were a fly on the wall in the home where you think the grass is greener, you would most likely be trying to get back to your side. Satan tried to convince Me to accept his offers to turn the stones into bread, to jump from a tall building so the angels could catch me, and he offered Me all the world's kingdoms. Everything Satan offered was already Mine. Satan dresses up his offer, but you already have what is being offered. I blessed you with all the green grass you need; do not envy what others have. Just be happy with what I present you. You will be surprised to know that others think your grass is greener. ***Peace and blessings.***

Peace And Blessings : with the Risen *SON*

Day
Three Hundred and Twenty Four

Born to Die

Luke 9:23 (NIV) "And he said, "The Son of Man must suffer many things and be rejected by the elders, the chief priests and the teachers of the law, and he must be killed and on the third day be raised to life." We created man in our image, made perfect, and placed him in the Garden of Eden to live. Man sinned by eating the forbidden fruit. I left heaven on a mission from my Father to mend the broken relationship between man and my Father. I was born to die a sacrificial death as a lamb on the altar. I knew I would be crucified, a terrible death for any person to face. My death would be necessary because no human was sinless and could fulfill this task. I am being sacrificed for man's sins. At my death, a priest is no longer required to atone for man's sins. The veil in the temple was torn down; now you have direct access to me without a priest. On the third day of my death, I rosed with all power, and now I sit beside my father in heaven.

I was born to die for your sins and your salvation. Do not let My death for your sins be in vain. Accept Me as your Savior while you have time. ***Peace and blessings.***

Peace And Blessings : with the Risen *SON*

Day
Three Hundred and Twenty Five

Sin is Sin

When one sins, their relationship with Me is broken. Sin is falling short of My glory or deliberately violating My will. When you die, your soul is separated from the body and returns to Me to render judgment. If you go to an earthly court, some individuals request conviction for a lesser crime. In My eye, sin is sin. There is no little or big sin. Stealing a pen is the same as killing another person. The penalty is the same, which is death. When you come to Me for judgment, once I decide your fate, there is not a lesser plea to request. There is no one or no higher court to appeal your case to. My Father, in his infinite wisdom, made a provision for you. He sent Me, born through the Virgin Mary, to live a sinless life on earth. I died on the cross as a sacrificial lamb for your sins. Accept Me as your savior and enjoy eternal life in heaven or eternal life in hell. Sin is sin, and hell is real. The choices you make have consequences; what is your decision?

Romans 3:23 (KJV) *Peace and blessings.*

Relationships

Day
Three Hundred and Twenty Six

When You Walked With Me

I watched over you last night. When you are at peace,
you have beautiful dreams. Dreams are so wonderful
that most of the time, you only remember the last one.
I want you to be at peace and to enjoy the splendor of
a beautiful relationship with me. As your Shepherd,
caring for you is a joy as you follow me. You have
no fear of your surroundings because of your faith in
me and the protection I give. Walking with me, you
are covered and protected from known and unknown
dangers. As you enjoy this new year, let nothing come
between us, and you will experience greater happiness
than last year.

"No weapon that is formed against you will succeed,
And you will condemn every tongue that accuses you
in judgment. This is the heritage of the servants of the
LORD, And their vindication is from Me," declares the
LORD." (NASB) *Peace and blessings.*

Peace And Blessings : with the Risen *SON*

Day Three Hundred and Twenty Seven

Choose This Day

Joshua encourages the Israelites that now is the time to choose who they will serve. His words transcend times and the people he addressed. Daily, you are allowed to enter My family of Christians. Do not worry about people talking about you because they will talk anyway. Base your decision on where you want your soul to spend eternity. Stop straddling the fence; you need to be on one side or the other. You cannot enjoy the sins of this world and worship me also. Do not let my suffering, death, and sacrifice for you be for nothing. Yoke with me, connect with me, walk with me, and enter a relationship you have never experienced. Enjoy my presence and an excellent relationship with me. My blessing to you for making the right decision. "And if it seems evil unto you to serve the LORD, choose you this day whom ye will serve; whether the gods which your fathers served that were on the other side of the flood or the gods of the Amorites, in whose land ye dwell: but as for me and my house, we will serve the LORD." Joshua 24:15 (KJV) ***Peace and blessings.***

Peace And Blessings : with the Risen *SON*

Day
Three Hundred and Twenty Eight

Oops, That Slipped

When you write on paper, you can erase what you wrote. When you type on the computer, you can backspace, highlight, and erase what you typed. But once you speak words, you cannot reach out and take them back.

Words have tone; you know how one can inflate or put their attitude into what is being said. When speaking, be careful of the tone or attitude that can be read in what you say. Seek forgiveness quickly and try not to be a repeat offender of the same offense. Look at my words in the sermon on the mount in Matthew 5. They were calm and effective in motivating the people. Consult with Me through your reading and meditation before you speak.

Control your words before they exit your lips. Choose your words carefully so you do not have an oops of the tongue. "But the tongue can no man tame; it is an unruly evil, full of deadly poison." James 3:8 (KJV)
Peace and blessings.

Peace And Blessings : with the Risen *SON*

Day
Three Hundred and Twenty Nine

Your Christian Gait (walk)

How is your walk with the Lord? People can identify you by your gait. Your gait has rhythm and movement, which is seen in your walk. Take a moment and review your spiritual gait. Are you still walking with me, or have you slid off the path? Continue walking with Me. Call on me to help you get back on this critical path. Get back on the path quickly because the longer you are off the path, the further away from Me you will walk. Reading the Bible shines a light on the path you should be on. I know what you face, and I have prepared a way to bring you through; walk with Me. Just follow the Light if you are too far away to see me. "But if we walk in the light, as he is in the light, we have fellowship with one another, and the blood of Jesus his Son cleanses us from all sin." Gait is a particular way or manner of moving on foot." 1 John 1:7(EVS)
Peace and blessings.

Peace And Blessings : with the Risen *SON*

Day
Three Hundred and Thirty

Your Lense

A lense is a glass or transparent substance with curved sides for concentrating or dispersing light rays, used singly in a magnifying glass or with other lenses, as in a telescope. (Oxford Dictionaries) My definition of a lens is how you see things. Do you understand what you see, read, or hear correctly? Do you need to look again, reread, or ask someone to repeat what they said? How do you see me from what you read in the Bible since I am not physically present? Am I just a name in the Bible, a former prophet, or do you see and accept me as your Savior? Through your lens, you bring clarity to your trust and faith. Please get to know me so I can cleanse your lens so you can see, learn, and understand me better (clearly). When you see me face to face, we will have unhindered fellowship. The view through your lens has a significant impact on our relationship. Look at Me more closely through a magnifying glass. "For now we see in a mirror, dimly, but then face to face. I know partly, but then I shall know just as I am known." 1 Corinthians 13:12 (NKJV) *Peace and blessings.*

Peace And Blessings : with the Risen *SON*

Day
Three Hundred and Thirty One

Synergy

Synergy is the interaction or cooperation of two or more organizations, substances, or other agents to produce a combined effect more significant than the sum of their separate effects. Church ministries are a variety of organizations whose synergy or interaction must be a collective effort to promote Me, Jesus as Savior. Working together makes a unified force supporting one another and fighting Satan, our enemy. Note to ministry leaders: Satan's mission is to divide and conquer. United, you stand but divided; you will fall. Being united includes being in the home, at your job, and church. Put your synergy to good use. "Do not stop him," Jesus said, "for whoever is not against you is for you. "Luke 9:50 (NIV) "Whoever is not with me is against me, and whoever does not gather with me scatters." Luke 11:23 (NIV) *Peace and blessings.*

Peace And Blessings : with the Risen *SON*

Day
Three Hundred and Thirty Two

Sun vs. Son

The sun is a star at the center of the solar system whose diameter is about 864,000 miles, or 109 times that of Earth. It provides light and energy for the universe. I, Jesus, am the second person in the Godhead, and I gave My life to reconcile the broken relationship between man and God. God (Father, Son, and the Holy Spirit) created the sun. The sun is bright, but I am the light of the world. The planets rotate around the sun, while your relationship with God evolves around Me. The sun is reflected off the water while I walk on it. The sun is the hottest at noon, but I started doing My Father's will at 12. The physical sun rises in the east and sets in the west, but I will come from the east and shine on the world. The sun has a corona resembling a crown of thorns during a solar eclipse, but I wore a crown of thorns before being crucified. When I died, darkness covered the Earth, and the sun bowed or failed to shine. You see the comparison of the sun to the son: walk in My light, enjoy ***Peace and blessings.***

Peace And Blessings : with the Risen *SON*

Day
Three Hundred and Thirty Three

Who Are You?

It is said that every person has three "selves." Having three selves means they have three sets of personalities, traits, beliefs, abilities, etc. The first type of self is the ideal self. The ideal self is the type of person that you want to become. The second type of self is the actual self. The actual self is who you are as a person. The third type of self is the perceived self. The third self is how you view yourself or who you think you are. Jim Rohn's old saying is that you are the average of the five people with whom you spend most of your time. As you look at the above information, it makes you consider your category.

When you give your life to me by accepting me as your Lord and Savior, you will become the right person. Your challenge of trying to become is over because the Holy Spirit is there to lead you into being the vessel Our Father desires you to become. Walk with US (Father, Son, and Holy Spirit) and not ahead of US; your life will change, and your identification will become known because you will grow into everything God wants you to be.

"Before I formed you in the womb I knew you," Jeremiah 1:5a (ESV). ***Peace and blessings.***

Peace And Blessings : with the Risen *SON*

Day
Three Hundred and Thirty Four

Birds of the Same Feather

The phrase "Birds of the same feather flock together" literally means that birds that belong to the same species will form a flock together. Nevertheless, this proverb is symbolic: it refers not to birds but to people. Birds of the same feather flocking together means similar people will get along and do things together. It may remind you of a clique; you find cliques in every organization, including the church. People with the same likes, thought patterns, desires, goals, achievements, sororities, fraternities, and culture tend to hang together. But what about Christians? Do you associate with Christians you do not know at other church gatherings or those from your church? As the title states, you may fall in line with birds of the same feather. Christians are of the same feather because of your connection to Me. If I am your center, then we should be able to recognize other birds of our species (other Christians from various locations) to fellowship with, pray with, and worship. If not, you may need to change feathers because I do not and will not change.

"Do not be deceived: "Bad company ruins good morals. "I Corinthians 15:33 (NET) *Peace and blessings.*

Peace And Blessings : with the Risen *SON*

Day
Three Hundred and Thirty Five

Stay in Your Lane

New drivers are nervous and work hard to stay in their lane. But this phrasing pertains to more than driving. You leave your lane when someone is driving and try to drive as a passenger. You are out of your lane trying to tell someone how to do something you do not have the skills or knowledge of. You are out of your lane when you tell your pastor how and what to preach. When you drift into others' conversations, giving unrequested advice and giving your unrequested opinions are examples of getting out of your lane. When this happens, confusion starts.

The confusion begins on the job, at home, and church when individuals leave their lane. When you stay in your lane, there is less traffic, confusion, and no division. God is not the author of confusion. Stay in your lane, do your job, and the church will operate more smoothly. Stay in your lane in all facets of your life for less confusion. "That there should be no schism in the body, but the members should have the same care one for another." 1 Corinthians 12:25 (KJV).
Peace and blessings.

Peace And Blessings : with the Risen *SON*

Day
Three Hundred and Thirty Six

Hospitality

Hospitality is the friendly and generous reception and entertainment of guests, visitors, or strangers. Some people love to entertain and have guests. Each culture has different methods of what is considered entertaining. In this COVID environment, fun can be more challenging. Your attitude sets the stage for how relaxed and entertained your guest feels. Attitude is the key ingredient. Our text reminds us that we could be entertaining angels who represent God. Treat them harshly if you dare. However, the caveat is that you never know who an angel is; therefore, you should be courteous and treat everyone nicely. You never know what blessings await you from the treatment you give to others. Do unto others as you would want to be treated. "Be not forgetful to entertain strangers: for thereby some have entertained angels unawares. "Hebrews 13:2 (KJV) *Peace and blessings.*

Day
Three Hundred and Thirty Seven

If You Love Me

Stevie Wonder sang "If You Love Me." These are potent words often stated in relationships. These words are paramount in maintaining a holy and righteous lifestyle in our relationship with God. Sometimes, statements are made to test your love.

I did this with Peter. If you love me, it challenges the depth of one's love for another. And then the caveat or the stipulation comes: if you love me, treat me better; if you love me, put your love into action; if you love me, help me with the children; if you love me, clean up after yourself; if you love me let's agree to disagree; if you love me, forgive me; and I said if you love me to keep, My commandments. The Bible shares three types of love: Eros, Philia, and Agape, with Agape being the greater of three because it's unconditional. I want your unconditional love and for you to keep My commandments. It's challenging, but you can do it, don't you agree? "If you love Me, keep My commandments. "John 14:15 (NKJV) *Peace and blessings.*

Peace And Blessings : with the Risen *SON*

Day
Three Hundred and Thirty Eight

What's Your Legacy?

Solomon writes an essential message to his readers, both past and present. As Solomon is reviewing his life, he finds so many vain things. He has labored and acquired riches, building beautiful homes, storage buildings, and even a temple. In all the wisdom Solomon gained, he realized that even he must die. His physical legacy (treasure, buildings, possessions) must be passed on to someone. Solomon says, who is to say if this person is wise or a fool; regardless, it is passed on to someone.

You are just like Solomon, trying to teach your children the importance of what you have built for them. Most do not want it because they want to live in the legacy they have not built. Tell your children to live in your legacy until they can develop their own. What is the spiritual legacy your children recognize in you? Are they ashamed or proud of you? It is not too late to make them proud and, more importantly, yourself. Let Me assist you in redefining. And who knows whether he shall be a wise man or a fool? Yet shall he rule over all my labor wherein I have labored and shown myself wise under the sun. This is also vanity. "Ecclesiastes 2:19 (KJV) *Peace and blessings.*

Peace And Blessings : with the Risen *SON*

Day
Three Hundred and Thirty Nine

Things Taken for Granted

What do you take for granted as if it will always be available? Your wealth, health, family, and availability to talk with God. When you become complacent, you overlook your beautiful surroundings, your families, and the many blessings I give you. Take a moment to tell someone you love them, slow down, and appreciate the simple pleasures in life and live. The things that are chores in life are the things you hate to do. You ever wonder if forgiving humankind is a chore for Me. Thank Me for being a forgiving Savior.
Peace and blessings.

Peace And Blessings : with the Risen *SON*

Day
Three Hundred and Forty

Deal or No Deal

"For God so loved the world that he gave his one and only Son, that whoever believes in him shall not perish but have eternal life." John 3:16 (NIV) You have read this verse many times. What did you perceive from it? My Father sent me to a world filled with sin that broke a wonderful relationship with Him. He loved His creation so much that He sent Me to become a sacrificial lamb to redeem, renew, refresh, and restore a broken relationship. I was without sin. No human was worthy of this task because all humans had sinned. Once my sacrifice was completed, all you had to do was accept me as your lord and savior, that is the belief in Him part. In doing so, you gained access to eternal life. Do not let the world's view and non-belief in Me be a factor in your salvation. When I check the Book of Life and your name is absent, you will not have a place in my kingdom. RSVP while you have time.
Peace and blessings.

Day
Three Hundred and Forty One

Witness

A witness has first-hand information and is who was present to see or hear for themselves. The writers of the gospels had first-hand knowledge of some of the things they wrote about, and there were times they relied on the testimony of others. Sometimes, you must read each writer's story to get the complete picture. What do you know about me? Do you rely on what others say or see for yourself? You must have first-hand information to witness me. Maybe you can witness me healing your body, or when I calmed your fears when you were having an anxiety attack, how I removed that excruciating headache, or when you called on me when your child came out of the closet. There are things you can witness to others about me if you are not ashamed of me or the situation. For whosoever shall be ashamed of me and my words, of him shall the Son of man be ashamed, when he shall come in his glory, and in his Father's, and of the holy angels. Stand up and be a witness of Me.
Peace and blessings.

 Peace And Blessings : with the Risen *SON*

Day
Three Hundred and Forty Two

Creatures of Habit

Have you noticed how habitual you are? In the home, some of you leave the dishes to clean in the morning, leaving at the same time, taking the same route to work every day, stopping at the exact location for your favorite coffee or breakfast sandwich, taking the same parking space at work, you schedule your smoke breaks at the same time to be with the same people, you do the same for lunch, and you arrive home at the same time daily. Do something different. It may surprise you that a number of people know your schedule, but they are not connected to your Find My Phone app. It's time to break that pattern because Satan knows your pattern, what turns you toward sin, and how to initiate it. What is your spiritual life pattern, your walk with Me, Jesus?

Your spiritual relationship with Me must not be broken. Increase what you are doing spirituality to keep Satan at bay, making you a more challenging target, and Satan will seek a softer person to persuade to sin. Remember, if Satan presents you with an opportunity to sin, I will provide you a way to escape; please take it because I did not leave or forsake you. Become a creature of habit in your spiritual relationship and enjoy the blessings I send. *Peace and blessings.*

Peace And Blessings : with the Risen *SON*

Day
Three Hundred and Forty Three

A House Divided!

A single thread breaks easily. However, combining two or more threads makes it more challenging to break. A house divided is the devil's Joy because he can rip it apart by keeping spouses fussing over something as simple as which way to put the toilet paper on the roll. Toilet paper rolls can be an issue until you use the bathroom without tissue. At this point, just having tissue would be great. Congeal your home by renewing your relationship with your spouse and children. Do not give Satan a ride because he's determined to drive. Note to you: "There is only one steering wheel." A house divided cannot stand. The slightest turmoil becomes an earthquake inside the home. Reconnect with Me, and I will say, "Peace be still, " remove the storm, earthquake, or turmoil, and bring happiness back. When spouses connect, congeal, work together, and become one, that thread is so strong that Satan will depart and look for a weaker target.

Please walk with Me and not ahead of Me to avoid taking the wrong path into the storm. I see the future much better than you can.: "And if a house be divided against itself, that house cannot stand." Mark 3:23 (KJV) *Peace and blessings.*

Peace And Blessings : with the Risen *SON*

Day Three Hundred and Forty Four

A House Divided, Pt 2

To divide and conquer is Satan's way of destroying togetherness. He divides by causing confusion and putting out false statements, better known as half-truths. He does this even in church. Sheep will drink from still waters and settle without parasites, flies, or friction. If a church is known for fighting among themselves, having money problems, heated church meetings, teaching false doctrine, or a disruptive spirit, new members will not join, and present members will leave. The closer your church grows in its meditation and conversations with me, the quicker I will heal a divided church.

The church is the individuals, not the building. During COVID-19, each member had a chance to get closer to Me because I took away the building. Members walk with Me more while others try to lead ahead of Me. As God, I should lead them. I may have to give them a depraved mind and walk away from them. The song says, "Lord, if you lead me, I cannot stray." A divided church will not grow, causing many members to miss their heavenly journey. Congeal (come together) spirituality to grow physically and spiritually. "And if a house is divided against itself, it cannot stand. "Mark 3:25 (KJV) *Peace and blessings.*

Peace And Blessings : with the Risen *SON*

Day
Three Hundred and Forty Five

Teach us to Pray

The disciples asked Jesus to teach them to pray. With such an honorable request, Jesus gave them an example. He started with "Our Father" to address his petition to the highest authority, God the Father. Jesus recognizes where His Father is located, which is in Heaven. Hallowed or holy is thy name. Wow, what a fantastic introduction.

Prayer is like a letter; it has an opening where you address whom you are sending the letter to or prayer, in this case, a body, which is your request or petition, and a closing. Jesus is teaching his disciples, as well as present-day disciples, how to pray. Take time and practice writing your letter to God. "After this manner, therefore, pray ye: Our Father which art in heaven, hallowed be thy name. Matthew 6:9 (KJV) "*Peace and blessings.*

Peace And Blessings : with the Risen *SON*

Day
Three Hundred and Forty Six

Mr. Harper's Prayer

While conducting my duties at a Rest Home in Durham, NC, Mr. Harper, a resident there, blessed me with a prayer called "Thanks to God." Hello God, I called tonight to talk for a little while. I need a friend who will listen to my anxiety and trials. You see, I can't make it through a day alone. I need your love to guide me so I will never feel alone. Please keep my family safe and sound. Come, fill their lives with confidence for whatever fate they're bound to. Give me faith, dear God, to face each hour throughout the day and not worry over things

I cannot change. Thank you, God, for being home, listening to my call, and giving sound advice when I stumble and fall. Your number, God, is the only one that answers every time. I never got a busy signal and never had to pay a dime. So, thank you, God, for listening to my troubles and sorrows. Good night, God. I love you, too. I will call again tomorrow! *Peace and blessings.*

Day Three Hundred and Forty Seven

Worship

Pray this prayer. Father, I honor You and worship You. There is none like You. I will rise and sing praise to You. I will take every opportunity to keep the relationship we have built in a place of reverence through worship. Psalm 95:6 says, "Oh come, let us worship and bow down; let us kneel before the LORD, our Maker!" I bow to You, Oh God. There is no one that compares to You! *Peace and blessings.*

'

Day Three Hundred and Forty Eight

Relationships

When you sin, you hide from the one you hurt, but more importantly, you hide and decrease or stop communicating with God. The irony or funny part of this is that God already knows what you have done, who you did it to or with, and where you are hiding. Lol. Sin broke the relationship with God for Adam and Eve; it does the same for you. Sin is a barrier, a wall, a deterrent that breaks relationships in the home, at work, with friends, and with Me. You must tear down this barrier quickly to restore broken relationships. You restore by seeking forgiveness as the sinner and forgiving as the forgiver. Work hard to maintain unbroken relationships with Me and others.

"And they heard the voice of Jehovah God walking in the garden in the cool of the day: and the man and his wife hid themselves from the presence of Jehovah God amongst the trees of the garden." Genesis 3:8 (AVS)
Peace and blessings.

Peace And Blessings : with the Risen *SON*

Day
Three Hundred and Forty Nine

Avoid Confusion

My sheep will only eat or stay where there is peace. People will leave your church of worship seeking a peaceful location. Be aware of individuals who create controversies, disagreements, or things that hinder the progress of the Christian faith. These individuals promote themselves and not the "Good News" of the Bible, which is Me, Jesus Christ. In most of these situations, the confusion is initiated by members trying to seize or obtain the power they do not have at home or work. Remember, I have all power; do not persecute My church. Reestablish order and collectively as a body, hold my hand and walk with me.

"Now I urge you, brothers and sisters, to watch out for those who create dissensions and obstacles contrary to the teaching you learned. Avoid them!" Why is there confusion in the church? I am not the author of confusion but of peace and harmony. Romans 16:17 (NIV) *Peace and blessings.*

Peace And Blessings : with the Risen *SON*

Day Three Hundred and Fifty

Wrong Stands Out

Wrong stands out; therefore, avoid, bypass, or go around evil, sinful things and people. Cling or attach yourself to godly people who have your best interest in mind.

If godly people are avoiding you, then you need to evaluate the perception you are advertising. Re-evaluate, reconsider, or renew your relationship with Me to ensure you are displaying Christ-like characteristics. Others are watching you, so be sure they see Me in you, and I will draw others to me. Remember, wrong stands out. "Beloved, follow not that which is evil, but that which is good. He that doeth good is of God: but he that doeth evil hath not seen God." Watch ye; therefore, you do not know when the Lord shall call your souls away. (KJV) 3 John 1:11 *Peace and blessings.*

Day
Three Hundred and Fifty One

The Inner Circle

When Jesus traveled, the multitude and his disciples
followed him. But when Jesus needed time alone, he
usually took James, John, and Peter, whom he recognized
as his inner circle. Why were these three so close to
Jesus? Were they more attentive to Jesus's parables? Did
they ask more questions, or did Jesus have unique plans
for them? Let me ask you the right question. Do you have
an inner circle? Who is in your inner circle? Will they tell
you when you are wrong or agree with you to keep the
peace? Do you have confidence, trust, and faith in your
inner circle? Are these your prayer partners whom you
can call on at any time to pray? I invite you to become
members of Jesus' inner circle. In your inner circle, you
block out your surroundings and focus on Jesus, and
Jesus will lead, guide, teach, and pray with you and show
you the path to an everlasting union with him. Please take
this opportunity to get closer than close to your Savior.
How do you get there? Intensify your Bible reading,
studying, and prayer life; your life will change.
Peace and blessings.

Peace And Blessings : with the Risen *SON*

Day
Three Hundred and Fifty Two

Communication with the Father

Prayer is one of the greatest tools to connect with Me. In prayer, you bring your concerns and requests to me with honesty and openness. This discipline shows Me that you truly desire to connect with Me. Be consistent with this practice. Stepping away from your day and take moments to connect with Me. I tell you in My word to pray without ceasing! Praying to Me is like picking up a phone and dialing the only one who can calm the storm, bring healing and restoration, and more. Today, I challenge you to find moments to steal away and pray to Me.
Peace and blessings.

Day
Three Hundred and Fifty Three

My Brother's Keeper

As I look around and absorb the facts and events around me, I find that no one wants to be their brother's keeper. There is no concern as to the condition of others. When walking down the pathway of life, someone is subject to stumble and fall. Are you there to pick that individual up, or are you standing back laughing? That could have been you. What does it take to know we are our brother's keepers? Ethics is doing what is right and moral even when no one is looking. Do you do what is right only when it is in your favor? Yes, you must be careful when helping others since society has changed; therefore, ask Me who can you assist so that you will effectively work in the scheme of My plan. Just like Jesus, you are servants first. Wow, am I doing a good job being your brother's keeper? In that thought, I am somebody's brother also. "And the LORD said unto Cain, Where is Abel thy brother? And he said, "I know not: Am I my brother's keeper?" Genesis 4:9 (KJV)

Peace and blessings.

Peace And Blessings : with the Risen *SON*

Day
Three Hundred and Fifty Four

Restore a Fallen Christian

"Brethren, if a man be overtaken in a fault, ye which are spiritual, restore such a one in the spirit of meekness; considering thyself, lest thou also be tempted." Galatians 6:1

This scripture is significant to being a disciple. It says to restore a fallen Christian, you must restore one who is lost to win them to Christ. Restoring one who is lost shows them the Christ in you. You restore by forgiving and assisting them in seeing the error of their ways. If the truth is told, sometimes it is easier to restore the lost verses a Christian. Often, the Christian is in denial, not wanting others to know they fell or sinned. Get up, brush yourself off, and employ your resilience. But all have sinned and fallen short of the glory of God. Nothing is new under the sun, so help a brother or sister restore or gain them back to Me. I do not want this to happen, but if you should be tempted and fall, hopefully, another Christian will assist in your restoration; it is your Christian duty. Do unto others as you would have them do unto you; RESTORE one another and stop spreading rumors. *Peace and blessings.*

Peace And Blessings : with the Risen *SON*

Day
Three Hundred and Fifty Five

Save the Date

I'm sorry that the date you must save is
not on your calendar. It is not an imaginary date but a
date where no man knows the day or hour of My return.
It is not a date you are saving, but you are preparing for
a journey with no beginning or end date. You do not
have to pack a picnic basket of food; gas is not required
since transportation is provided. No unique clothing is
needed, so do not pack a suitcase. Are you preparing
for the third part of your salvation that "when the Lord
returns, the Christian will be saved from all the physical
results of sin and of God's curse on the world?"
My return will be a joyous time for those who have
prepared for this great day. Save the date by looking
beyond what this world offers and look toward the
heavens as you work on a closer relationship between
you and God. Although the date is unknown, do not
become complacent; continue to build and improve your
relationship with Me. SAVE THE DATE!
Peace and blessings.

Peace And Blessings : with the Risen *SON*

Day
Three Hundred and Fifty Six

The Unseen Battle

The spiritual war that we face started when Lucifer wanted to take over heaven. Michael and his angels fought and defeated Lucifer and his angels. The war you fight on earth is spiritual. A war that is not seen by the naked or natural eye. It takes a spiritual person with discernment to see and understand this war. You have Me, Jesus and the Holy Spirit to assist you in winning your spiritual battles, but you must be willing to follow Our instructions. Look beyond the person giving you problems and see the guidance and influence of Satan on their actions, words, and deeds. Just as Lucifer was thrown out of heaven, Jesus, the Holy Spirit, and I can throw him out of your life. " And there was war in heaven: Michael and his angels fought against the dragon, and the dragon fought and his angels, and prevailed not; neither was their place found any more in heaven. And the great dragon was cast out, that old serpent, called the Devil, and Satan, which deceived the whole world: he was cast out into the earth, and his angels were cast out with him." Revelation 12:7-9 (KJV): *Peace and blessings.*

Peace And Blessings : with the Risen *SON*

Day
Three Hundred and Fifty Seven

Get Right with God

I will judge everyone by the authority given to Me by God the Father. Some do not believe in the resurrection of life or judgment, but God has forewarned you. Some individuals view society's judge and jury process as a joke, but I, Christ, is the jury and judge; My decision is final, and there is no appeal. Encourage others, but remind yourself to get right with God and do it today.

Tomorrow is not promised because your tomorrow could be your today. I remember a song, "Get right with God, and do it now, get right with God, He will show you how. Right down at the cross, where He shed His blood, get right with God, get right, get right, get right."

Enjoy your day in the Lord. "And he has given him authority to execute judgment because he is the Son of Man. Do not marvel at this, for an hour is coming when all in the tombs will hear his voice and come out, those who have done good to the resurrection of life, and those who have done evil to the resurrection of judgment." John 5:27-29 (ESV) *Peace and blessings.*

Peace And Blessings : with the Risen *SON*

Day Three Hundred and Fifty Eight

The Perfect Church

The Holy Spirit gave Peter knowledge of who I Am. Peter's mission and your mission is to seek the lost and present them an opportunity to accept Me, Jesus, as their Lord and Savior. The challenge is getting the unsaved to not focus on the physical church as the perfect church on earth. Once you enter any church, you consider perfect; it loses its perfection. A pastor once told me that if you find an ideal woman, walk away, and don't bother or touch her because she will no longer be perfect once you do. His thoughts were the same about a perfect church on earth. It is through Christ that you can obtain perfection in heaven. So, keep others from your high standards. Your standards are not perfect; they are your standards. "And I say also unto thee, That thou art Peter, and upon this rock I will build my church; and the gates of hell shall not prevail against it." When reading this scripture, one may believe that Peter is the rock Jesus speaks of. But the rock is the words "You are the Christ, the Son of the living God." Matthew 16:18 (KJV) *Peace and blessings.*

Peace And Blessings : with the Risen *SON*

Day
Three Hundred and Fifty Nine

Engagement

"Now the birth of Jesus Christ was as follows: After His
mother Mary was betrothed to Joseph, before they came
together, she was found with child of the Holy Spirit."
Matthew 1:18(NKJV)

Betrothed means engagement. Each culture has a different
respectful period of engagement. Some individuals meet
on the Internet and get married in a few weeks. In the case
of Joseph and Mary, their betrothed period was one year.
They lived together as Joseph became a future husband
and provider during this time. Can you understand his
bewilderment since he did not have sexual contact with
Mary, and now she was pregnant? Could you survive a one-
year engagement living with your future spouse and not have
intercourse? If either were to have a sexual relationship with
another person while engaged, they could be stoned to death.
If you are married or engaged, take your commitment very
seriously because even today, there are consequences.
Peace and blessings.

Peace And Blessings : with the Risen *SON*

Day
Three Hundred and Sixty

You Were Once Them

"For we ourselves also were sometimes foolish, disobedient, deceived, serving divers lusts and pleasures, living in malice and envy, hateful, and hating one another. But after that, the kindness and love of Me, your Saviour, toward man appeared." Titus 3:3-4 (KJV)

Paul is expounding to Titus, whom he left in Crete to manage the church. He reminds Titus and you of your previous life of sin and some of the things you were doing, just like the people of Crete. You see the fault in and of others forgetting about your life before you found and accepted Me as your Savior. As you matured in Me, you were once them. They who were disobedient, those who sought the various physical pleasures Satan presented, those who hated others, and Them who were disobedient, those who hated others, those whose existence was to enjoy a sinful life. Because you were once them, wrong stands out without looking for it. Do not think you are better than others (Them). Once you convert to a Christ-like life, your mission is to show, display, and tell others (Them) about the goodness of Me and the blessings they are missing that I have for them also. You became a disciple; now lead "Them" to Me. Lead the new way.
Peace and blessings.

Peace And Blessings : with the Risen *SON*

Day
Three Hundred and Sixty One

Building a Relationship

Pray this prayer: Father, I thank You for giving me such a foundation in You. This relationship that I have committed to over the last several months has shown me how valuable You are to me. I thank You for this relationship that we have established and the foundation that You have laid for me. I commit to keeping You at the forefront of my world and staying true to the plan and purpose You have spoken over my life for You are a friend that sticks way closer than any other person ever could. Thank You for loving me today and forevermore.
Peace and blessings.

 Peace And Blessings : with the Risen *SON*

Day
Three Hundred and Sixty Two

You Must Prioritize Me

In order to connect with Me, I have to be the most important thing in your life. You have to make sure that you have placed me in my rightful place. I prioritized you when I sent my only Son to die on the cross for you! I prioritized you when I allowed Jesus to endure humanity just so you could have an option to choose Me. How crazy is that? Because of my love for you, I gave up everything and still allow you the option to choose Me. But if you want to build a relationship that will stand forever. You have to prioritize Me. So as you go throughout your day, make sure I stay in the forefront of your mind. Truth be told, you are always on mine! *Peace and blessings.*

Day
Three Hundred and Sixty Three

My Love Language

I love to be Worshiped! It is one of the reasons creation
was made. And when you learn the way I like to be
loved, it gets my attention! My love language is found
in worship. Worship Me. Call upon Me. When you rise
in the morning tell Me how much you have need of Me.
I want to hear the praises of My people. I want you to
focus your mind on Me and allow My Spirit to lead and
guide you. I want you to spend time in My word and
explore new ways to speak to Me in My love language.
Peace and blessings.

Day Three Hundred and Sixty Four

A Prayer of Consistency

Pray this prayer with Me. God, I honor You. I thank You for the love You show me each and every day. I thank You for showing up consistently in my life and in the lives of those connected to me. You have been such an accountable God, exemplifying how I should show up in relationships. You have shown me how to prioritize the right things and value connection so much that I, too, show up consistently.

Help me to be the best version of myself. I pray that my consistency increases and my trust in You is elevated to another level today. Holy Spirit, pull the reins if I go too far left or right. Allow me to stay within Your perfect will. ***Peace and blessings.***

Peace And Blessings : with the Risen *SON*

Day
Three Hundred and Sixty Five

Jesus is the Light

Can you imagine a star leading the wise men to me, baby Jesus? The star led the wise men to the light by the light to see the world's light. The wise men were led to me by a light to see the heralded messiah, the savior of humankind. What led you to me? Was it your inquisitive nature to see if what was talked about was true? When you connect with me, I can light up your world. The word is a lamp for your feet, a light for your path. I would love to shine light into your life and guide you on a path that can lead you to my kingdom. Just as the wise men followed a star, allow me to be your shining star, and your life on earth will change. When I shine light into your life, walk with me, and I will be your shepherd, your protector. Do something different today: walk beside me, not ahead but beside me, and watch what happens as I lighten your path. "That was the true Light, which lighteth every man that cometh into the world." John 1:9 (KJV) *Peace and blessings.*

Peace And Blessings : with the Risen *SON*

Translations

Understanding the Translations Used in this Devotional

This section is designed to help readers understand the various Bible translations used in this devotional. Although there are many translations, these translations represent the message conveyed in the devotional.

When reading one of these devotionals, a translation is not shown; it is the King James Version (KJV).

Word for Word - Adhering to the words and structure of the original language without sacrificing clarity. The translations below meet the word-for-word standard.

ASV American Standard Version
CSB Christian Standard Bible
ESV English Standard Version
HCSB Holman Christian Standard Bible
KJV King James Version
NKJV New King James Version
NIV New International Version
NET New English Translation

Thought for Thought - Thought for thought is prioritizing clarity and understanding of the original language's meaning without sacrificing accuracy.

NLT New Living Translation

Meet the Author

Rev. Booth earned his Bachelor's degree in Business from the University of Management and Technology in Arlington, VA. His passion for scripture led him to pursue and complete a Master's Degree in Divinity from Shaw University Divinity School, graduating in May 2016. He was ordained on January 8, 2017, and completed his Clinical Pastoral Education at Rex Hospital that same year.

With a distinguished military career spanning thirty-seven years, Rev. Booth retired as a Command Sergeant Major. He is a veteran of both Desert Storm and the Iraqi wars. Notably, all soldiers under his command returned home safely, a testament to his leadership and divine protection.

Called by the Lord to teach, counsel, and expand the Kingdom through missionary efforts, Rev. Booth is dedicated to sharing the gospel, offering salvation to the unsaved, and encouraging the faithful to trust the Lord wholeheartedly.

Rev. Booth and his wife, Deborah, have been married for 34 years and are proud parents to Kellie Booth Wright (Brentley) and William Booth II (Lacey). They are also blessed with three grandsons: Jaden, Justice, and William Booth III.